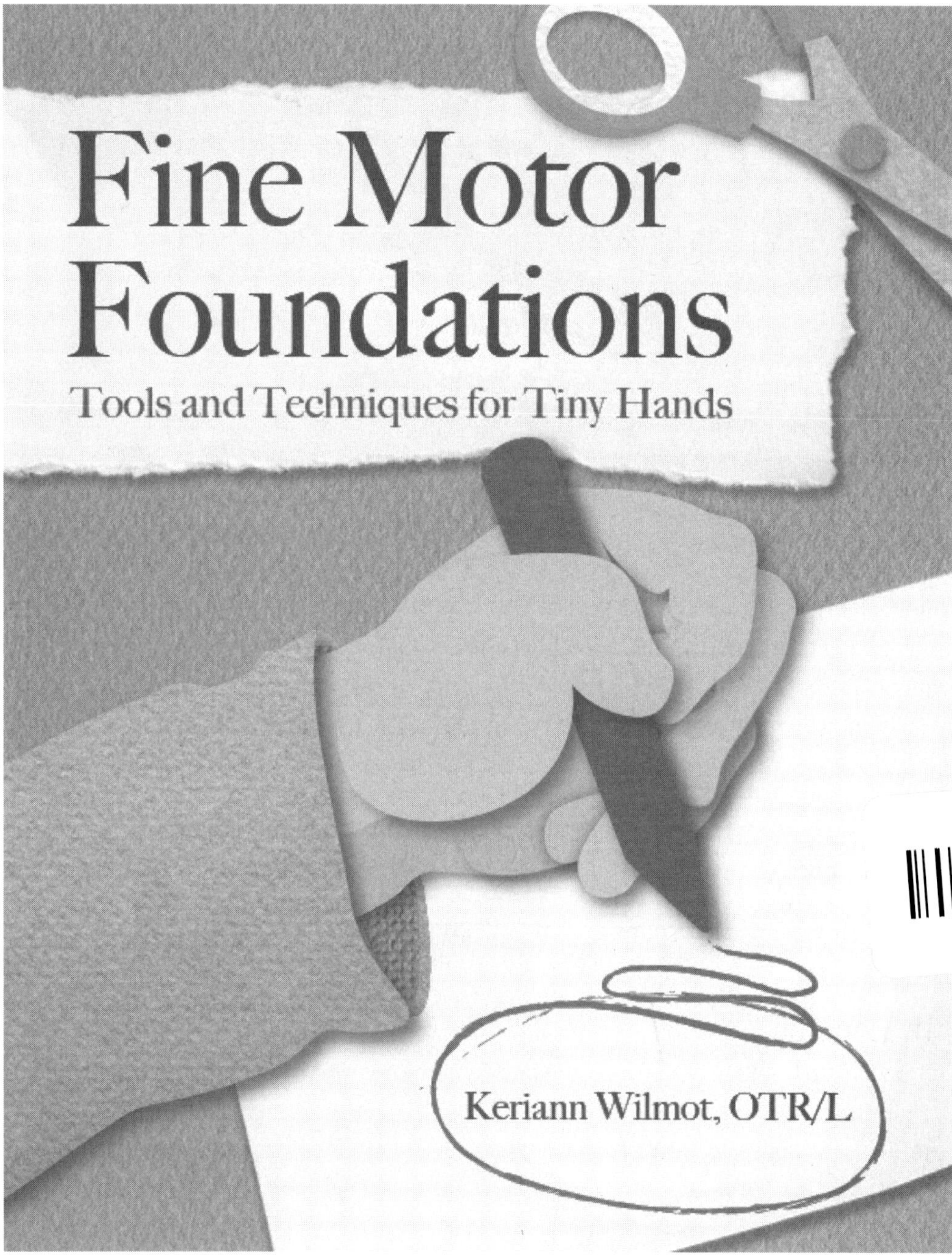

Gryphon House
www.gryphonhouse.com

Copyright

Published by Gryphon House, Inc.
P. O. Box 10, Lewisville, NC 27023
800.638.0928; 877.638.7576 [fax]
Visit us on the web at www.gryphonhouse.com.

Library of Congress Control Number: 2024932351

Bulk Purchase

Gryphon House books are available for special premiums and sales promotions as well as for fund-raising use. Special editions or book excerpts also can be created to specifications. For details, call 800.638.0928.

Disclaimer

Gryphon House, Inc., cannot be held responsible for damage, mishap, or injury incurred during the use of or because of activities in this book. Appropriate and reasonable caution and adult supervision of children involved in activities and corresponding to the age and capability of each child involved are recommended at all times. Do not leave children unattended at any time. Observe safety and caution at all times.

Table of Contents

Preface

As a pediatric occupational therapist (OT), I'm often asked general questions like, "What are fine motor skills?" And more often than not, to avoid over complicating it, my response is something quick such as, "It's pretty simple. They're how kids use their hands to play, write their name, and engage in everyday skills, like eating with a utensil, getting dressed, and tying their shoes." Now, after finishing this book, I think you will agree with me, that these intricate skills that children are developing from the time they are born and well into adulthood are complicated, extraordinary, and amazing. Fine motor skills play a role in just about every single activity we do, each and every day.

I share the quote above because I feel that, for me, it really captures the wonder of development. How a baby grows in utero, then within just a few short months after birth develops the strength and coordination needed to talk, walk, and use their hands to play is not impulsive. Development is natural, consistent, and happens along a predictable timeline. These little steps seem to happen effortlessly, with so many tiny details that most people don't even pay attention to. The steps will all come together over time to create the foundational skills needed for the individual to achieve their potential.

There is a lot of information shared in this book about fine motor skill development, and I'm sure it's overwhelming. Unless you are or plan on becoming an OT, please don't worry about memorizing the names of every possible fine motor skill or grasp pattern. They are there as a reference. I recommend familiarizing yourself with the skills of the age group you teach and interact with. Look at the photos of the different grasp patterns, and just use your observation skills to watch how children use their hands to play. Knowing what's expected for the children you interact with will help you to spot the child who could benefit from some additional strategies and interventions.

There will be situations where OT and more consistent help through therapy will be important, but it's not always easy for families and children to get support right away—or at all. Even with an efficient process, it can take months to get a child established in therapy. So, think of how much of a difference you will make by providing quality learning experiences in your classroom or playroom, even if it's something as simple as breaking your regular crayons in half and adding a few pairs of loop scissors to cut with.

Often, I see that the toys in a classroom or in a home don't fit the developmental levels of the children. Sometimes, the toys are too simple and children get bored quickly; other times, the toys and activities are so advanced that children don't participate for very long. The moment an activity feels like work and isn't fun, they are off to find something else that motivates them.

I've spent a fortune on toys over the course of my twenty-five-year career. Over the last fifteen years, I've prioritized finding the best to use in my everyday experiences as part of therapy with children. I've worked side-by-side with toy companies in the product-development process, and my expertise and understanding of play have been sought by toy companies all over the world. I know a lot about the types of educational toys and activities children really love to play and engage with.

Please reference the lists of companies and toys I've included in the book to help you make informed choices about the types of toys and activities you are offering to the children you work with each day. But I totally get it: toys and technology are expensive, and not all schools have budgets to support buying new ones. This is why I want to make sure that there are ways to make your own activities using simple household items too!

Thank you so much for reading this book, I'm positive you will use what you've learned to make a difference in the lives of the children you support each and every day. I love to educate others and am always available for trainings, webinars, and events. Please share your success stories, and ask me any questions you have. Feel free to reach out to me here:

www.KeriWilmot.com
On Facebook: @ToyQueen
On Instagram: @Keri_Wilmot
On LinkedIn: @KeriannSullivanWilmot

Acknowledgments

Thank you so much to my husband, Derek, who didn't get scared off when he met me twenty years ago and saw that drove around in a car with a trunk full of toys. Instead, he's found creative ways to support and encourage me to share my knowledge and passion so more parents, teachers, children, and even toy companies from around the world can learn practical ways to promote play.

To my son, Gavin: Keep working hard. When you are passionate, doors you never thought existed will open for you. Being your mom and advocating for you has motivated me to continue to educate as many teachers and parents as possible, so that all children, no matter their skill level, can improve their performance and confidence.

To my current and past clients and your outstanding parents and families: When your child needs occupational therapy, it's not usually a club you want to belong to. Thank you for inviting me into your homes and sharing your stories. You've given me the priceless gift of experience.

To my mom and dad, family, friends, co-workers, and everyone I've met through the ToyQueen.com community over the years: The opportunity to write this book would not be possible without your support.

Introduction

"Great things are not done by impulse but by a series of small things brought together."

—Vincent van Gogh, artist (attributed)

Think about the last time you saw a child captivated by squeezing playdough through a press, finishing a jigsaw puzzle, or even drawing a self-portrait complete with different body parts and a hat, glasses, or a hairstyle that is unique to their appearance and personal interests. Children make playing with toys by using their hands look so easy and fun. When development occurs naturally and as expected for a young child, these complicated skills become automatic and effortless.

The development of various life skills is crucial for a child's future success (both academically and socially) and independence. However, people often try to predict a child's future success based on a few major developmental skills, such as how quickly the child learns to walk, talk, and become potty-trained. Additionally, when children start preschool, the focus is often on how fast they learn their colors or write their names. But using both hands together in a coordinated way is much more important than many realize. Our hands help us to do everything! How else would we tie our shoelaces, eat with a fork and knife, or hold a phone to text our friends?

Did you know that the key fine motor skills we focus on in preschool actually start developing in the womb (Martinez, Dugdale, and Conaway, 2023)? Some lucky expecting families see this development in action while watching their baby suck their thumb on the monitor during an ultrasound. After birth, babies continue to develop, use, and refine these skills until adulthood. Here are some examples of how humans continue to hone their fine motor skills throughout life:

- Babies use fine motor skills within the first few weeks of life by bringing their hands together while they are being held, then quickly learn to reach out for their parent's nose or lips while being breastfed or drinking from a bottle.
- Toddlers pick up small pieces of food off their plates or trays to eat, and they learn how to hold and drink from sippy cups. Their play skills develop over time as they learn to twist open the tops of containers, complete puzzles, scribble with crayons, and cut with scissors.
- By kindergarten, children are learning to write their names, tie their shoelaces, and zip up their coats.
- Elementary school–aged children use forks and knives to cut their food.
- Teenagers and adults use fine motor skills every day to take notes, text friends, or type emails.

As you'll see demonstrated throughout this book, it is vital for children to develop good eye-hand coordination and hand strength early on, as these abilities have a tremendous effect on the success of children's academic experiences years later.

My Qualifications for Writing This Book

As a pediatric occupational therapist (OT), I feel so lucky to have had a career working with young children for more than twenty years. At this stage of my career, I've spent a minimum of forty thousand hours helping to improve the lives of children of all ages, mainly through play, at their homes, in day cares and preschools, and in hospitals through evaluation and treatment. I'm excited to share with you why the skills I address in this book are so important, along with the tips, tricks, and ideas I've learned along the way to make building these skills fun for young children.

My work as an OT allows me to observe children through a lens that dives deep into a child's skill development. While I'm looking for age-appropriate skills to get a sense of whether a child has a delay, my training enables me to look at the underlying skills children need for complicated tasks and to offer practical solutions for improving their performance. So, for example, I monitor and check off on my list whether a child can put on their socks and shoes and tie their shoelaces. If the child can't, I can provide more insight as to why. Is it that the muscles in their hands are weak and the child gets too tired? Is the child distracted and not paying attention to the instruction?

Even though I (and other OTs) might identify deficits in a child's development, I use a strengths-based approach to build skills positively. Evidence-based practices and research help me choose the right interventions to help children make progress. Then, I put an action plan in place to help, based on the child's individual deficits.

From the moment I started working with children, I began collecting the toys, games, and activity ideas that I thought would be most helpful in supporting children's skills. Because of my passion for finding quality educational toys, in 2009 I began sharing online and through social media practical ways to play. I have built relationships with every major toy company and serve as an expert resource to toy industry professionals, where I'm known as the "ToyQueen," because I have personally reviewed, engaged with, and written hundreds of articles on toys, games, play, and development for children of all ages and abilities. I have served as a judge for the Toy of the Year in the United States, and for many years I have rated and judged toys for the ToyAward, a prestigious award given to only a few toys each year at Spielwarenmesse, a prominent international fair in Nuremberg, Germany.

I am constantly incorporating new toys into my practice, sharing my reviews and items through social media and on television segments, and I can't wait to share some of my classic favorites in this book. I'm always looking for the best items that are not only motivating and helpful for children but are also budget friendly and provide exceptional play value.

Working with children of all ages and abilities has given me some valuable information, which I'm going to share directly with you to help you make confident decisions and informed choices for the children you work with.

A Little Bit about Occupational Therapists

As an OT, I look at a person's ability to complete "activities of daily living." These are skills people need to perform every single day on their own, such as getting dressed using fasteners such as zippers and buttons; brushing their teeth thoroughly; tying shoelaces; and using utensils to scoop, pierce, or cut food. Performing these actions successfully requires that individuals have many underlying foundational skills, such as strength, coordination, control, and problem solving. As pediatric OTs, our profession is instrumental in helping children achieve these skills, if needed, from the day they are born into early adulthood.

OTs help individuals learn the skills to do their jobs or occupations in the settings that are appropriate for their age. For children, their "work" is to exhibit attention, strength, and coordination to play and learn at home, in community places such as playgrounds, and in their child-care facilities, preschools, and elementary schools. Pediatric OTs play a major role in teaching children how to focus on learning by using self-regulation skills and good coping skills, enabling children to perform their "jobs" to the best of their abilities. In addition, children need the right combination of strength and coordination to perform age-appropriate daily activities.

The clients or children we serve may have disabilities, diagnoses, delays, or medical conditions that affect their ability to achieve these skills. Consequently, to offer the support children need to make progress, OTs work in all sorts of places: hospitals, child-care programs, preschool programs, public schools, and community clinics and programs. Depending upon a child's age and which state they live in, we might be able to visit children at their homes to teach them these skills while also educating their family members on tips and tricks to work on these skills throughout the week. As much as possible, we help to foster inclusion by seeing children in their natural environments with other children their own age.

We make a difference in a child's life as early as the day they are born. Still, not many people are fully aware of the important roles occupational therapists play in helping children engage in their everyday activities. We are experts in developmental milestones, and our knowledge is valuable in helping children improve their skills to develop to their full potential.

Someone once asked me if the strategies that we use as therapists to help children with disabilities could be beneficial for typically developing children. Yes! As therapists, we first learn about typical development so we can support children who are struggling with certain skills. All the strategies we use are beneficial and can be applied to any child. Generally, development happens in a predictable path; some children just take longer than others to achieve these skills. No matter their age, the steps are the same.

Challenges with Fine Motor Skill Development

Over time, I've noticed that societal changes have contributed to fine motor skill deficits and other developmental delays, which makes it crucial to prioritize motor skills in early childhood settings. For example, babies need supervised "tummy time" to build head and neck control as well as upper-body and core muscle strength. But, in my experience, the design and production of trendy infant devices such as rockers, swings, and portable car seats has made it harder for some families to remember to give their babies safe play opportunities on the floor.

Children have access to portable tablets and cell phones for long periods. A study by Common Sense Media found that, in the years from 2011 to 2013, the percentage of children with a smart mobile device at home increased from 52 percent to 75 percent (Common Sense Media, 2013). In 2020, Common Sense Media reported that children ages two to four were logging two and a half hours of screen time per day; for children ages five to eight, screen time increased to three hours per day (Rideout and Robb, 2020). At early ages, many children prefer technology, tablets, and video games over traditional toys and games, affecting skill development through play. The Michael Cohen Group (2014) reported that touch screens occupied 65 percent of playtime for children ages twelve and under. The children preferred electronic devices over traditional toys, such as dolls and action figures, board games, puzzles, construction blocks, and arts and crafts.

This preference for electronics has caused problems with young children's fine motor skills. When accessing their devices to play games and watch videos, many children use their thumbs and fingers awkwardly. Tablet and device use alone do not build the solid foundational motor skills needed for pencil use in the elementary school years. When they start school, children have more opportunities to use technology and type and have fewer opportunities to handwrite.

The COVID-19 pandemic affected a lot of experiences for children in those important infant, toddler, and preschool years. Researchers Watts and Pattnaik (2022) found that children became dependent on their family members to help them with their daily life skills and that many teachers reported students exhibiting delayed fine motor skills in the classroom. These challenges, coupled with the trend toward push-down academics in the early years, mean that many teachers feel pressure to expose children to writing letters, numbers, and sentences before they enter kindergarten (Bassok, Latham, and Rorem, 2016; Moyer, 2020). Grasp and fine motor development norms have not changed; instead, research supports guided play as a more appropriate approach (Bassok, Latham, and Rorem, 2016; Taylor and Boyer, 2020). As preschoolers are exposed to developmentally inappropriate academic activities, such as writing letters before they are developmentally ready to perform these complicated motor actions, they can develop inefficient and awkward grasp patterns, poor writing habits, and frustration in general with pencil-and-paper tasks. This leads to negative behaviors and task avoidance.

How to Use This Book

This book is focused primarily on helping early childhood teachers, family members, teacher trainers, and OTs to support and improve children's fine motor skills, from birth through the early education years and kindergarten. The amazing part about development is that the steps happen along a timeline, or a continuum, in a predictable order. So, the information in this book can also help older children who exhibit delays in their elementary school years.

I encourage you to become familiar with the developmental skills of children at certain ages and within different settings and environments. With that goal in mind, I share developmental information and appropriate practices, but there is always more to learn. To improve children's skills and limit frustration, try to keep a mindset of promoting general development that is appropriate for a given child's age and the setting they are in. Because curriculum standards are not always aligned with developmental expectations, I share ways to modify activities to meet the needs of children and to support their learning and skill growth.

How This Book Is Organized

- Chapter 1 shares key information about general developmental milestones and appropriate expectations for different ages.
- Chapter 2 explains the complicated process of how the hand develops strength and skill; this information serves as a basis for understanding school-readiness grasp patterns in chapter 3. Chapters 4, 5, 6, and 7 explore visual motor skills, which are the specific eye-hand coordination skills needed to play with toys and engage in various self-care tasks, such as manipulating fasteners, using eating utensils, and tying shoelaces.
- Chapter 8 offers lots of tips regarding safely and accurately cutting with scissors.
- In chapter 9, we tackle how to improve a child's writing performance with handwriting curriculums and pencil-and-paper activities.
- Looking for ways to promote fine motor skills through apps and technology? We explore that topic in chapter 10.
- Including family members is a great strategy for providing practice and repetition for learning, so Chapter 11 includes ways to help promote fine motor skills at home.

- As occupational therapists, we have a unique ability to modify activities to help a child improve their performance, so throughout the book, I share some of my favorite tips to make activities easier or harder, as needed, to build skills and improve confidence.
- Interspersed throughout this book, I share case studies. These real-life examples show how adults use strategies and tools to help a child accomplish a fine motor task, such as cutting or coloring, in order to make positive changes quickly when a child shows immature fine motor skills.
- The book concludes with several appendices that list my favorite toys by skill or concept, toy companies committed to designing quality educational toys, a list of common items that can be used for simple fine motor activities, as well as a glossary of some frequently used fine motor terms to use as a reference.
- Text boxes highlight tools and toys I've found particularly helpful, along with suggestions on how to use them in your classroom or home.

Fine motor skills are so much more than holding a pencil to write letters and numbers; these skills are how children use their hands to play and complete daily activities. My goal is that you will learn to think differently about the tools and activities you choose each day, to provide children with the best possible experiences for each stage of their development.

While I have personally spent thousands of dollars on toys and games in my career, you do not need a large budget to effectively help children improve their fine motor skills. My goal with this book is to offer a variety of suggestions for items that you can purchase or even create using common household items.

You will see recommendations for specific brands of toys and items in this book. These are not paid placements. If a toy, game, or company is included, it's because I personally recommend those specific brands or items that I believe have outstanding benefits or qualities. Please beware of knockoffs and off-brand items from discount stores or even websites such as Amazon or Temu. While you could save a few dollars up front, over time you might notice a difference in a child's experience with or use of the product.

Thank you for wanting to learn more about helping children improve their fine motor skills. Children learn through practice, repetition, and exposure, and the time you spend researching activities, buying materials and toys, and playing with these toys and games alongside children will be beneficial.

CHAPTER 1:

A Snapshot of Early Childhood Development

Development, no matter the skill area, is all about achieving milestones along a continuum or timeline. For example, an infant first begins to smile at around six weeks old and at about one year of age is often walking, waving hello, and speaking a few unclear words. Within each area of development are different skill sets, such as gross motor skills, fine motor skills, language, cognition, and self-help skills. Within each skill set are hundreds of steps along the continuum that happen over the course of many years. In short, development generally moves forward from one skill to another. Knowing about typical childhood development will make it much easier to spot weaknesses, so you can start helping children advance their skills.

As you work with children, you will learn which skills typically develop at which times. If a child enters your classroom and is not yet doing the things their peers are doing, you likely will notice that the child might be developing more slowly than other children. For lots of reasons, which might include experience and opportunity, some children do progress a little slower. This might indicate a delay, or the child could actually be performing within a range of what is considered typical for their age group.

If something doesn't seem quite right, perhaps after a developmental screening, you might share that information with the child's family—not to diagnose an issue but to make the family aware. As an early childhood educator, it is not your role to diagnose a disability, but you can encourage families to find resources to get the help the child needs. Often, families will speak to a pediatrician to learn more, and the pediatrician will conduct their own screening. If a delay is present, early intervention is important to give children the support and help they need as soon as possible.

When a Child Has an Identified Delay in Skill Development

If a professional screening finds that a child does have a delay, the child might be referred to one or more specialized therapists. If a child has a delay in fine motor and/or self-care skills, they might be referred for occupational therapy services. If a child has a delay related to gross motor skills, such as sitting or walking, then they would be referred to a physical therapist. For language concerns, such as with speaking or understanding directions, the child would be referred to a speech pathologist. As therapists, we do our own testing, compare the results with the guidelines and checklists we have, and determine whether a child is performing within an age-appropriate range or is presenting with a delay so significant that it would be considered a disability.

If you are lucky enough to have a therapist visit your child-care or school classroom to work directly with a child, this can be an absolute gift! You might feel nervous and worried, but you'll feel better as you discover how helpful it is to have access to someone like an occupational therapist. The OT might bring toys and activities to help the children they work with. As a therapist, I give teachers and family members personalized activities to do that will help a child make progress. Often, those strategies will also benefit the other children in the classroom, too.

For children with developmental delays, some responsibility will fall on you to follow through with the OT's recommendations. When the OT is in your classroom, take advantage of the opportunity to watch how they interact and engage with children. Pass what you learn on to the child's other caregivers, because collaboration, whether at home or at school, will be the key to the child's success and progress. You will have the power and opportunity to make a tremendous difference in that child's development.

Prenatal Fine Motor Development

Can you believe that all the motor skills a person uses in their life start from the moment they are conceived and develop throughout the pregnancy? Here are some fun facts about the kinds of motor skills an unborn baby is developing. (Note that babies develop at their own rates, but these are the general time frames in which certain skills can be observed.)

According to Medline Plus (Martinez, Dugdale, and Conaway, 2023), a resource provided through the National Library of Medicine, a human typically follows a developmental timeline in the womb:

- **Around eight weeks' gestation:** The arms and legs are becoming longer, and the hands and feet are beginning to form.
- **Around ten to eleven weeks:** The hands and feet are formed, and finger- and toenails begin to form.
- **Around eleven to fourteen weeks:** The fetus can make a fist.
- **Around fifteen to eighteen weeks:** The fetus can move, stretch, and make sucking motions.
- **Around nineteen to twenty-one weeks:** The fetus can move around more and can swallow.
- **Around twenty-two weeks:** The fetus is more active with increased muscle movement.
- **Around twenty-three to twenty-five weeks:** The bone marrow begins to make blood cells, and the lower airways of the lungs begin to develop.
- **Around twenty-six weeks:** The eyes are developed, and the fetus may startle at loud noises. The lungs are not yet ready to function outside the womb.
- **Around twenty-seven to thirty weeks:** The brain grows rapidly, and the eyelids can open and close.
- **Around thirty-one to thirty-four weeks:** The bones are fully developed but still soft.
- **Around thirty-five to thirty-seven weeks:** The muscles and bones are fully developed.
- **Around forty weeks:** The baby could be born any day!

It is absolutely amazing that a baby begins to develop all the necessary motor skills for life while growing inside their mother. So, what changes after a baby is born? They need to perform all the same skills they learned in utero, but they now have to complete them against the force of gravity, without support from the amniotic fluid in the womb. Depending on the skill, it can take months, if not years, for a child to progress through the various stages of fine motor development. Life experiences and other considerations such as genetics and predisposition to other diagnoses can also affect skill development.

But what happens if babies are born prematurely, earlier than thirty-seven weeks? Children who have not had the time in utero to develop these skills will still need to do so after they are born. This is often why premature babies are in the hospital for a bit of time after birth while they adjust to the world and all its stimulation. They continue to grow and develop, just outside of the womb now. When children are born prematurely, they are at risk for many medical complications that might affect their future development. In fact, they are at risk for developmental delays in all areas, so they are often monitored by doctors and therapists for many years. To make sure these children stay on target with their skills, some families connect with OTs and other specialists right after a preterm birth, then engage in services almost immediately when discharged from the hospital. Premature babies will usually have their developmental milestones more closely monitored than babies who are born full-term without complications. Keep in mind, however, that children born prematurely do not necessarily exhibit delays.

CDC Milestone Tracker

The Centers for Disease Control and Prevention (CDC) offers a free website and app that can help families and early childhood educators monitor children's developmental milestones. Both the app and the website include free screening tools, activities, and suggestions on what to do if there are concerns for children from birth to age five. You can find the website here: https://www.cdc.gov/ncbddd/actearly/milestones/index.html

After a baby's birth, doctors monitor development, such as whether the baby can suck effectively to eat and gain enough weight, whether they are moving their arms and legs, and how they handle the stimulation of the world. As children age, pediatricians and family doctors monitor specific categories of development from birth into adulthood. These include areas such as the following:

- **Cognition:** the skills for a child's ability to pay attention, to remember details and sequences, and to solve problems creatively and quickly with good processing speed
- **Communication:** the ability to follow verbal instructions and to use sounds and words to communicate wants and needs clearly
- **Social-Emotional:** how children engage and interact with siblings, peers, parents, and teachers
- **Gross Motor:** skills that require strength and coordination in larger muscle groups, such as walking, jumping, and climbing, so children can explore their environment

- **Fine Motor:** skills that require strength and coordination of the smaller muscle groups of the arms and hands to perform daily activities such as writing, eating with utensils, and tying shoelaces
- **Self-Help:** a child's independence with daily activities such as getting dressed, eating, toileting, and completing chores

General Developmental Skills by Age

Before we can really understand fine motor skills, there are some general developmental principles we need to keep in mind. Child development is complicated, and many of these areas—including fine motor skills—depend on and affect other skill areas. When you look through the following examples, you'll see some crossover from fine motor skills into other skill areas. A doctor or therapist evaluating a child's developmental skills often will need to observe the child using fine motor skills to demonstrate proficiency.

- Evaluators often test children's cognitive skills by observing children using toys such as puzzles, problem-solving with blocks, or drawing with a crayon. If a child has difficulty with their fine motor skills, using those toys and materials will be challenging. Consequently, the evaluator will not get an accurate sense of a child's strengths and weaknesses in their cognitive skills.
- If a child is asked to follow a verbal direction, such as, "Please throw your snack wrapper in the trash," to evaluate their receptive-language communication, that child will need to use their gross motor skills to get to the trash can and their fine motor skills to open the lid and throw the item away.
- If a therapist is evaluating a child's self-help skills, such as eating with utensils or putting on clothes and fastening zippers and buttons, that child will need to use fine motor skills to perform these actions with ease.

The next section of this book provides a timeline of some important developmental milestones in each of the skill categories we've discussed; these milestones serve as a baseline for understanding what children can do at each stage of development. Keep in mind that the skills listed are the general developmental guidelines for children who do not have a diagnosed physical or developmental disability. Many disabilities, such as autism, attention-deficit hyperactivity disorder (ADHD), and learning disabilities, are not diagnosed until a child is older. But when families reflect upon a child's early development and compare their performance to these lists, they often recognize some skill areas in which the child was exhibiting a delay or slower development.

For children who do have identified disabilities, these milestones can serve as an excellent guideline to find "next steps" to push toward. However, these children may need special considerations, as they may not achieve all these exact milestones, might skip some, or might develop some out of order. Skill areas do not develop in isolation, so children can be building skills in different areas at the same time.

Infant (Birth to One Year)

So much happens in the first year of life! It's extraordinary how many skills children learn at such a young age.

Cognition Milestones

- Using skills to explore toys with senses (taste, touch, smell, sound, sight)
- Object permanence, or the ability to find a hidden object that moves out of sight, such as food underneath a napkin
- Imitating gestures such as clapping and waving
- Improving attention to play

Communication Milestones

- Alerting to sounds, including responding to their name by looking at the speaker
- Babbling with consonant and vowel sounds (such as *mama*, *dada*, or *gaga*) and saying a few single words
- Using sign language, such as banging their hands together for *more* or swiping away with both hands for *all done*

Gross Motor Milestones

- Rolling
- Sitting
- Crawling
- Pulling up to stand
- Standing
- Walking
- Jumping
- Climbing stairs or on the playground
- Transitioning from one position to another, such as moving from sitting to crawling

Fine Motor Milestones

- Visually tracking, or following people and toys with their eyes
- Holding, shaking rattles
- Exploring sensory features of toys with their hands and mouth by gripping, mouthing, shaking, and banging the toys
- Transferring toys from one hand to the other
- Pushing buttons on toys to activate lights and sounds
- Demonstrating a palmar grasp: using all five fingers to pick up and hold onto toys such as blocks
- Using hands with coordination to put or release toys into and out of containers
- Demonstrating a pincer or tip pinch grasp with the thumb and index finger to pick up foods

Self-Help Milestones

- Holding and drinking from a bottle and sippy cup
- Finger feeding themselves small, soft foods
- Taking off their socks
- Moving arms into the sleeves of shirts and legs into pants during dressing

Social-Emotional Milestones

- Quieting and calming in response to a caregiver's voice and touch
- Bonding with caregivers
- Smiling
- Playing peekaboo and blowing kisses

Toddler (One to Three Years)

Toddlers are mobile young children who walk, run, and explore their environments. Children of this age are improving their attention spans and playing in more complicated ways than before.

Cognition Milestones

- Putting items into toy cars and pushing them around
- Engaging in pretend play using toy kitchens, dolls, and similar objects
- Improving attention span to play with toys for longer periods on their own

Communication Milestones

- Pointing to pictures in books
- Talking in short phrases and sentences to communicate wants and needs
- Following two-step verbal directions

Gross Motor Milestones

- Walking up and down stairs while holding the railing
- Using ride-on toys
- Jumping
- Climbing
- Throwing a ball
- Kicking a ball
- Catching a large ball

Fine Motor Milestones

- Stacking blocks, imitating block designs
- Holding or stabilizing a container with one hand while the other hand puts items in or takes them out
- Scribbling and imitation of vertical and horizontal lines with crayons and markers, starting with a pronated grasp pattern and transitioning to a fingertip grasp pattern (We will learn more about grasp development in chapter 4.)
- Completing foam-board puzzles
- Beginning sensory play with playdough, paint, and sand
- Putting together construction toys, such as Duplos
- Using two hands to string beads

Social-Emotional Milestones

- Having separation anxiety from caregivers
- Participating in parallel play or playing next to (but not with) peers their age
- Imitating other children's motor actions while playing

Self-Help Milestones

- Using a fork and spoon to eat without spilling
- Drinking from an open cup
- Putting on and/or taking off socks, shoes, and other simple clothes
- Toileting skills
- Brushing teeth
- Combing hair
- Completing simple chores, such as throwing an item in the trash or using a wipe to clean a table

Preschool (Three to Five Years)

Many preschool-aged children begin attending school for a few hours per day and engage in school-readiness activities to prepare for kindergarten.

Cognition Milestones

- Developing color, letter, and number identification
- Imitating adults as part of play
- Learning their body parts
- Solving problems through building and construction play with 3D designs
- Using abstract thinking
- Learning about danger and responding to safety-related redirection, such as when an adult explains that an item is too hot
- Including three or more body parts when drawing a person

Communication Milestones

- Listening to stories
- Asking who, what, and why questions
- Using sentences with four or more words
- Being understood by others when talking
- Answering questions about their day

Gross Motor Milestones

- Running with coordination
- Participating in physical activities, such as swimming, soccer, or gymnastics
- Pedaling a small bike
- Balancing on one foot
- Hopping
- Catching a small ball
- Kicking a ball at a target

Fine Motor Milestones

- Imitating a circle or cross with a marker or crayon while using a static tripod grasp with their fingertips (See chapter 4 to learn what these grasp patterns look like.)
- Coloring inside the lines
- Using scissors to snip, cut on lines, and cut out simple shapes, such as a square or circle
- Imitating and creating 3D block designs
- Creating art projects with coloring, cutting, and gluing
- Playing board games
- In-hand manipulation, or maneuvering and managing small objects in their fingertips
- Holding a pencil with a tripod-style grasp pattern (See chapter 4 for more information on this grasp pattern.)

Social-Emotional Milestones

- Participating in cooperative play and pretend play alone and with friends
- Separating from their family to go to school
- Being able to comfort others
- Understanding expectations of behavior in different places

Self-Help Milestones

- Managing fasteners such as buttons and zippers
- Putting on their coat
- Using a dull knife to cut soft items

School Age (Five Years and Older)

Children ages five and up are ready to enter kindergarten, where they will often attend school all day and engage in learning activities such as counting, early literacy skills, and using pencils to write their names.

Cognition Milestones

- Exploring environments such as community playgrounds and play spaces
- Participating in group activities, such as library story time, with supervision
- Solving problems
- Engaging in fantasy play using their imagination
- Paying attention for five to ten minutes

Communication Milestones

- Telling a story with details
- Having conversations

Gross Motor Milestones

- Trying organized sports, such as soccer or baseball
- Running with speed

- Skipping
- Playing target games with a ball

Fine Motor Milestones

- Writing their name
- Using a mature tripod-grasp pattern on their crayons (See chapter 4.)
- Cutting out small shapes accurately with scissors
- Drawing detailed pictures of people with realistic proportions
- Completing puzzles with ten or more pieces
- Following directions to put together construction toys
- Completing art projects by following a model
- Playing board games with rules

Social-Emotional Milestones

- Following rules
- Taking turns
- Exploring the environment
- Developing friendships

Self-Help Milestones

- Tying shoelaces
- Cutting with a fork and knife
- Brushing teeth
- Wiping thoroughly after toileting

Underlying Skills Needed for Fine Motor Control

Now that we have a general understanding of a child's motor development and when they typically learn various skills, let's take a closer look at other factors that affect a child's fine motor skills, including vision, sensory development, cognition, and core muscle strength.

Vision

Vision is an important foundational skill needed for fine motor skills. *Occupational Therapy for Children and Adolescents* (Case-Smith and O'Brien, 2015) states that, at birth, an infant can see black, white, and gray colors best. Newborns are nearsighted, which means they can see only up to about twelve to eighteen inches from their faces. Within the first few months of life, babies begin to track. This means they can focus on a face or a toy that is moving from side to side or up and down in horizontal and vertical movements. Around the same time, babies begin to purposefully reach toward nearby items, such as toys dangling above them from an activity gym. They will also reach toward their family members' faces during nursing or bottle feeding and might even begin to look at and observe their own hands. As babies get older, they see more colors, and their vision becomes clearer. Vision will help them to navigate the world by motivating them to roll, crawl, stand, and walk.

In addition to visual acuity, or the ability of the eyes to see clearly at near and far distances, a few additional visual components affect fine motor control as children develop their skills. Visual motor skills are the ability to coordinate both fine motor grasping skills and visual skills, allowing a child to perform complicated activities such as noting the differences between shapes or pictures in books. Coordination and control are needed for stacking block towers, stringing beads, using utensils to feed themselves, and, eventually, writing with a pencil.

Doctors typically test children's vision at birth and at routine checkups; school systems may offer vision testing as well. This type of testing can determine whether a child might need to wear glasses if they do not see clearly. Vision evaluations look mainly at visual acuity. However, for children to develop visual motor skills, the eyes also need to focus on and track moving items. In the school-age years, these skills are important for using the hands to complete complicated activities such as holding a pencil and then writing their name with accurate sizing and cutting with scissors.

Children with suspected vision issues should be referred to an ophthalmologist, who can determine whether a child might need glasses or other forms of intervention to improve their vision. Children who have trouble seeing may have a hard time with eye-hand coordination, and sometimes their performance can improve quickly just by wearing glasses.

Sensory Development

In my first book, *Wired Differently: A Teacher's Guide to Understanding Sensory Processing Challenges*, I go into detail on how sight, taste, touch, hearing, and smell are important in a child's development. Three additional senses—vestibular, proprioception, and interoception—relate to balance, body awareness, and understanding body signals such as pain and hunger.

Infants first use their senses to explore. For example, their touch, or tactile, sense explores the textures and shapes of their toys. The auditory sense is stimulated with sounds such as music, crinkles, and bells. As discussed previously, vision plays a role in a child clearly seeing their toys and the environment. The sensory input motivates most infants to use their fine motor skills to meet their personal sensory needs. They use their fine motor skills to help them self-regulate. For example, infants suck on their hands to calm themselves when upset or to show they are hungry. And as their fine motor skills improve, they will hold toys and bring them to their mouths to bite and chew, especially to soothe their gums during teething.

Over time, children develop sensory integration, which is where all those complicated senses work together in harmony so children can engage with activities throughout the day in a focused way. Some children, however, display poor self-regulation because they cannot manage all their sensory systems. Some children may be easily distracted by a fluorescent light, a scent, the texture of a shirt, or noises. Others may need proprioceptive input, so they crash into people or objects or stomp around the room. Children with vestibular issues may struggle with balance; those with interoceptive issues may have a hard time knowing when they are hungry or thirsty or need to use the bathroom. Many children who struggle with sensory integration will refuse to participate in daily activities or be unable to focus on playing for long periods to develop their skills. This can lead to behaviors that affect their play and engagement, which in turn can cause difficulty in developing fine motor skills during their early childhood years.

Cognition

Once babies master the sensory aspects of engaging with a toy, they begin to tap into their cognitive or problem-solving skills. Cause-and-effect interactions are one of the first skills to develop. This is why babies love simple activities and find enjoyment in repeating them over and over again. Babies like using their cognitive skills to push a button to make a toy pop up or to activate flashing lights or music. When they engage with these activities, babies get feedback—sometimes positive, sometimes negative—and this teaches them how to start problem solving.

Strength and Postural Control

It may seem odd to connect strength and postural control to cognitive development, but they are related. Strength develops starting with the muscles near the neck, upper back, and shoulders. Then, over time, children gain more strength in their backs and abdomens. Strength then develops toward their legs and feet as they begin to crawl, stand, and walk. This is why "tummy time" play is so important. As babies lie on their stomachs, they learn to lift their necks and heads against gravity and turn their heads from one side to another. Gradually, strength in their arms improves as they learn how to prop themselves up on their elbows while lifting their heads up against gravity.

Developmental skills also advance from proximal (near the core of the body) to distal (farther from the core). This means that a child needs to have strong and developed stomach, back, and shoulder muscles to sit upright and be stable. Once this happens, it's easier to develop the smaller muscles of the arms and hands, because this stable base allows children to use their hands to efficiently play and engage in daily activities in a more controlled and coordinated way. Babies start to develop their core muscle strength and upper-body strength within the first year of life, often at the same time as they progress through their gross motor milestones for rolling, sitting, crawling, pulling to stand, and walking. Having the opportunity to move both sides of the body at the same time allows babies to use both the right and left hemispheres of their brains simultaneously, too. Cue the exploration!

★ ★ ★

I know all those developmental milestones are a lot to process and understand. So much development happens in a short amount of time. Feel free to use chapter 1 as a reference to learn about the skills expected for the age group you are spending the most time with. If you see any gaps in children's skill development or worry about them having delays, chapter 1 will give you a place to start so that you can offer activities to work on the next developmental steps.

Now that you have a foundational knowledge about developmental milestones, let's move on to building strength. One of the biggest challenges OTs see with young children is a lack of muscle strength in their core area—meaning their pelvic, abdominal, and back muscles—and in their hands. This lack of core and upper-body strength leads to fatigue, which makes many children give up quickly on what they are doing. Chapter 2 includes lots of fun, simple ways to help children build strength. We also explore flexible seating options that can help children who are still working on developing strength to also build fine motor skills during play.

CHAPTER 2:

Building Core and Upper-Body Muscle Strength

A child's upper-body and core muscle strength correlate directly to fine motor development. In this chapter, we look at how children develop their core and upper-body strength, how that is connected to their fine motor skills, and how you can help young children develop these muscles through fun activities and exercises.

Developing Core Muscle Strength

As Case-Smith and O'Brien (2015) share in their book *Occupational Therapy for Children and Adolescents*, newborns have limited control over their bodies. As they grow, they begin to develop strength in their core muscles, which include the muscles of the abdomen, back, and pelvis. This development usually starts with seemingly simple movements. Tummy time plays a crucial role in this process; when placed on their stomachs, babies learn to lift their heads, strengthening their neck and upper-back muscles. Gradually, these activities lead to rolling over, which engages and strengthens the entire core. By the time they are about six months old, most babies start sitting up unassisted, a clear sign of stronger core muscles. This core strength is essential not just for sitting but also for crawling and, eventually, standing and walking. It is also important in setting the foundation for fine motor skill development. Weak core strength can negatively affect a child's ability to hold a pencil and perform tasks that require grasp strength, dexterity, and motor control.

Changes in the baby-equipment industry as well as in technology have affected how children develop their core strength (Avruskin, 2018). The designs of jumpers, bouncers, portable infant car seats, floor sitters, and swings, while convenient for parents and child-care providers, can limit children's experiences and opportunities to develop their core and upper-body strength. The resulting lack of core strength is sometimes referred to as *container baby syndrome*.

With the increase in the use of technology (particularly entertainment videos and apps on tablets and smartphones) by young children, many are engaging in less active play. Sedentary lifestyles can lead to obesity, generalized muscle weakness, and poor endurance—and, over time, to cardiovascular disease, diabetes, and hypertension in adulthood (Alotaibi et al., 2020; Park et al., 2020).

Adding muscle-strengthening exercises into a child's day through brain breaks, trips to the playground, or obstacle courses is a great way to help children not only self-regulate for attention but also to build their strength through fun and engaging opportunities. If it's suspected a child is lacking core muscle strength, the following section offers a few more exercises and activities for children (and adults, too). Many of these activities are also great for improving upper-body strength.

Core-Strengthening Exercises

In addition to strengthening the core, these exercises can improve children's posture, ultimately allowing them to sit up taller for longer periods without getting tired.

Plank

Invite children to lie on their stomachs on the floor. Demonstrate how to rest on their forearms with the head up and the trunk stable. Have the children try to hold this position for ten seconds. Repeat two or three times, with a short break between repetitions.

Wall Sits

Invite children to stand up tall with their backs against a wall. Show them how to gently bend their knees and lower their hips toward the floor, as if sitting in an imaginary chair. Have the children try to hold this position for ten seconds. Repeat two to three times, with a short break between repetitions.

Bridging

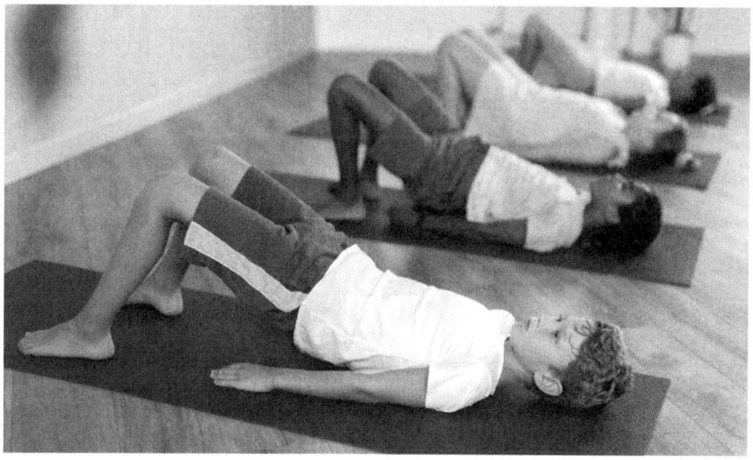

Invite children to lie on the floor on their backs. Encourage them to lift their bottoms while keeping their shoulders and feet on the floor, and to hold this position for ten seconds. Do this ten times in a row, with a short break between repetitions. As a motivator, sometimes it's fun to get a toy car or train and drive it under the children while they are holding their bottoms in the air.

Animal Walks

Children love to play imitation games such as Simon Says, so it shouldn't be too difficult to engage them in pretending to walk and act like different animals. These activities encourage children to take a variety of positions that allow them to use their arms and legs at the same time, in a coordinated manner, for a short period. These simple activities work on strength, endurance, problem solving, and motor planning as children try to figure out how to place their bodies in different positions. Ask them to move like lions, elephants, monkeys, crabs, frogs, kangaroos, bunnies, snakes—any animal you or they can think of.

Wall Push-Ups

Wall push-ups build core and upper-body strength. Invite the children to stand facing a wall. Encourage them to "push the wall" by flexing and extending their elbows while trying to keep their feet stable and the hands "glued" to the wall. Repeat ten times. Many children love pretending to use all their muscles to see if they are strong enough to "push the wall down." Encourage children to push for ten seconds, then take a break and try again. Children also love using different body parts, such as their sides, their bottoms, and their feet, to push the wall.

Obstacle Courses

Obstacle courses serve as a great way to build endurance as well as strength. They are not only fun but simple to create with basic, inexpensive equipment. They can include only activities that don't require equipment, but consider using items such as cones, painters tape, vinyl spot markers, scooter boards, plastic hoops, beanbags, a yoga ball, and a foam roller. Children can zigzag along a line of cones, walk along a strip of painters tape without stepping off, jump or hop to spot markers, sit on and move with scooter boards, hop or jump along a course of plastic hoops on the ground, toss beanbags at a target hoop, balance while sitting on yoga ball, and sit on foam rollers to do sit-ups or kick their legs. If the expectation is that children will complete the program for five minutes at first to build endurance, then over time slowly increase the amount of time spent at each exercise, so that the entire duration of the program is longer and the activities are more rigorous.

Don't have access to equipment? It's no problem. Here is an example of a simple exercise course to improve strength:

- Doing ten jumping jacks
- Holding a plank position for ten seconds
- Doing ten sit-ups
- Running in place for ten seconds

Children love designing their own combinations of three or four activities in succession. You will definitely need to help them at first, but over time you will see how confident they become in creating these courses. I often recommend completing each activity for ten seconds or ten repetitions before moving onto the next activity. If they cannot make up their minds or need some help getting started, providing small pictures that match certain poses or motor actions will make it easier for children to choose.

Movement Breaks

Children can build core and upper-body strength by participating in movement breaks that involve lifting their arms in the air to complete actions without resting. Some examples include dancing or imitating hand motions along with a song. No need to stress about being the center of attention when leading the group—websites and YouTube channels such as GoNoodle, MovetoLearnMS, and Cosmic Kids Yoga have hundreds of fun, short videos that will have children moving and dancing to build strength and coordination.

Developing Upper-Body Strength

Children need to build strength in all their upper-body muscles, which include the shoulders, biceps, triceps, forearms, and hands. In chapter 1, we discussed how upper-body strength starts to develop right after babies are born, especially when they begin engaging in daily activities such as tummy time. Strength continues to build through weight-bearing on their forearms and hands. Young children learn to move their muscles and sustain positions against the strong force of gravity. As they are learning to push through their hands to lift their heads, the muscles around the shoulder joints contract, which helps to build upper-body strength in the shoulders.

The progression of developing upper-body strength is visible in how an infant lies during tummy time. Early on, they lie with their head on the floor or bed, turned to one side. Then, they learn to use their neck to lift and turn their head from one side to another, push up through their hands, and begin to lift their head straight up. At first, the head bobs up and down because the baby lacks neck strength. As they get stronger, they can

keep their head up and steady while resting on their elbows and forearms.

When a baby can have a stable trunk position on the floor, they develop more control to reach. They may rest on one forearm while they extend their other hand to play with a toy in front of them.

From there, babies push up through their hands until they can support their body weight with their elbows fully extended. Rocking back and forth on their hands in this position is what builds the small muscles in the palms of their hands.

Babies learn to pivot in a circle on their stomachs, using their hands to pull. Ultimately, they use reciprocal arm movements to propel themselves forward, which is called *commando crawling* or *army crawling*. This allows them to use one arm, followed by the other, to pull themselves forward and backward while on their stomachs.

Babies then learn to push on their hands with full elbow extension while bearing weight on their knees in an all-fours position, which is also known as *creeping*. In this position, a baby will move one arm, followed by the knee on the opposite side of the body to travel forward short distances.

Once babies learn how to crawl, you will find them moving toward objects such as a couch or coffee table, then using their hands to pull themselves up to a standing position while holding on.

As babies develop into toddlers, they continue to build strength in their arms, using their hands to support their body weight, such as when they learn to crawl up stairs.

School-aged children continue to build arm and upper-body strength when participating in activities such as yoga or swimming and when climbing on play structures, rope ladders, monkey bars, and rock-climbing structures. In these activities, children use their arms to push, pull, hang, and support their body weight through both simple and complex movements.

Incorporating concepts into the classroom and daily routines that build upper-body strength is important for all children, especially for those who actually are exhibiting some upper-body weakness. The following are some fun ways to help children improve their upper-body strength naturally throughout the day, at home or in a classroom.

Using Vertical Surfaces

Completing a fun activity in which the child needs to consistently keep their arms at shoulder height or above is a great way to build upper-body strength and endurance. For example, consider taping coloring sheets to vertical surfaces such as easels, whiteboards, chalkboards, or bulletin boards instead of keeping the sheets flat on a desk. Using pocket charts with pointers can be fun for children as they help their teachers by pointing to letters, numbers, colors, or weather symbols.

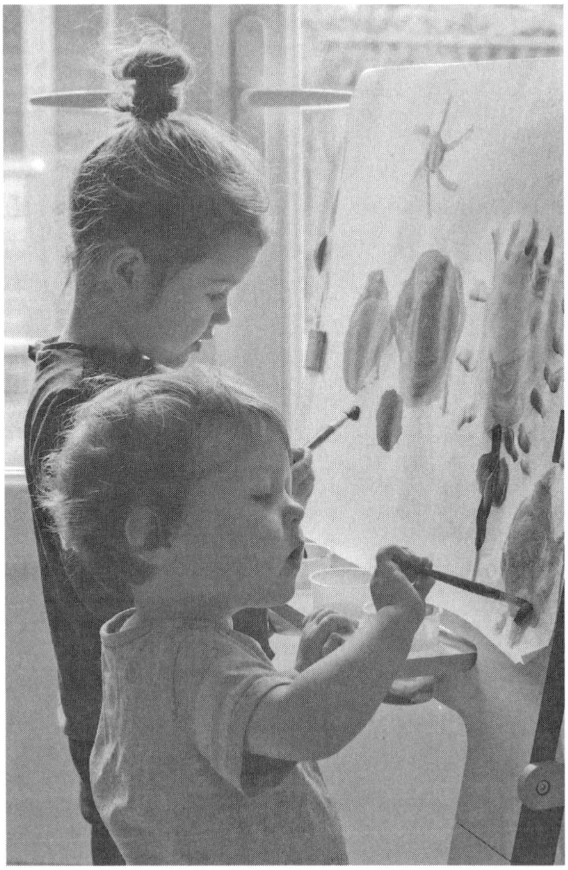

Playground Access

Climbing is a great way to develop upper-body strength. If you have access to a playground, encourage children to climb ladders, hold onto railings, and hang from monkey bars.

Vinyl Spot Markers

Durable, colored spot markers are useful for building core and upper-body strength and coordination. Place the markers on the floor in a line and use them for all kinds of activities that involve running, jumping, hopping, skipping, and galloping. They are great for children who are at different levels of strength and coordination.

- **Easier Activities:**
  - Encourage children to jump up and down on a spot marker with two feet.
  - Teach children jumping jacks. Have each child stand between two spot markers. Explain that when they jump, they can land with one foot on each marker, then jump again and bring their feet back together.
- **Harder Activities:**
  - Place spot markers in a zigzag pattern and ask the children to jump from one spot to another. Or, encourage children to hop on one foot from one spot to another.
  - Play a Twister-type game by calling out one color for children to put their hands on and another to put their feet on. You can also use dry-erase markers to write letters and numbers on the spot markers and play a similar game.

Targeted Upper-Body Strengthening Exercises

Some of the same core muscle-strength activities discussed earlier will also build upper-body strength. Those and the following activities can be incorporated into an exercise corner or done with the whole class during a movement break.

Plank

As described in the "Core-Strengthening Exercises" section, aim to hold the position for ten seconds, then take a rest and try again. Do two or three repetitions.

Pushing the Wall Over

Place both hands on a wall, and push hard against it for ten seconds without letting go.

Yoga Poses

Yoga poses are good ways to build upper-body strength, especially ones in which children are bearing their weight through their hands on the floor. Downward dog, for example, is a popular pose that helps to build upper-body strength. Hold the pose for ten seconds, rest, and repeat.

Lift-and-Carry Activities

Fill up two-liter soda bottles or gallon-sized jugs with colored water and glitter, then pick them up and move them from one location to another. Bringing in heavy groceries at home or delivering reams of paper to another teacher at school are other ways to build upper-body strength through lifting and carrying heavy items a short distance.

Sitting Posture

Sufficient upper-body strength and strong core muscles help children develop good sitting posture. The development of sitting posture begins in infancy as a baby is learning to sit upright against gravity, which happens at around six months of age. At first, babies will be flexed and hunched forward with their hands on the floor, and they will need the support of a person behind them to supervise and help them.

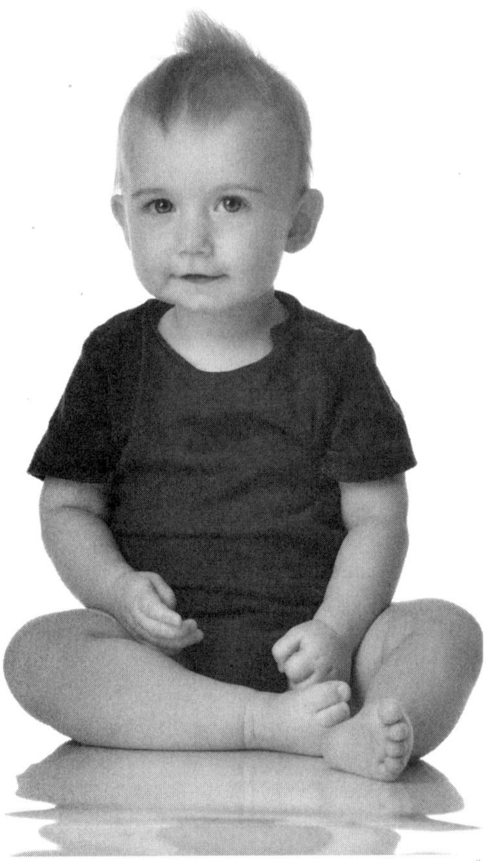

Then, over time, as the muscles develop, the baby can sit up taller while using their hands to play. Eventually, they develop enough strength to sit without falling over and won't need supervision. As children develop into toddlers, there will be some variations in how they sit while playing. A ring sit and a side sit are popular playing positions for young children.

One posture that needs to be monitored with young children is a W-sitting position, which is generally a sign of muscle weakness. Some children will continue to struggle with their posture even in their preschool years, and it will be noticeable, particularly on the carpet at circle time. Without the appropriate strength, they will sit with one hand on the ground, or they might shift their sitting position frequently, as if they can't get comfortable. W-sitting also affects children's ability to use two hands in a coordinated fashion while playing. Children who persistently W-sit might need a strengthening program to help improve their sitting posture.

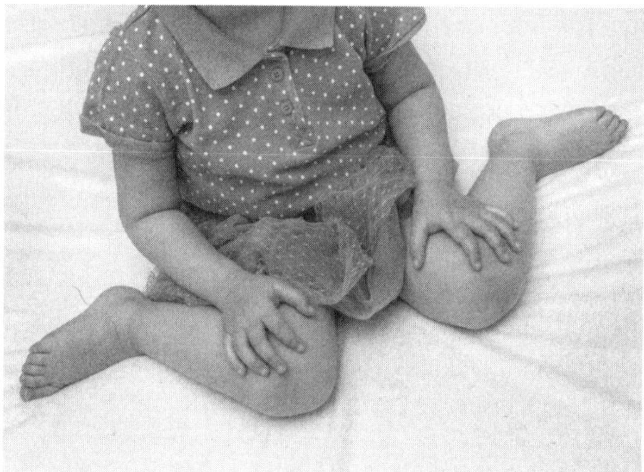

During circle time, teachers often ask children to "sit on their pockets" or "sit crisscross applesauce." There will no doubt be a few children who, no matter how hard they try, aren't able to sit in these positions. When children do not have the proper muscles to support their posture, they sometimes focus a lot of their energy on just trying to stay sitting up. This can lead to being unable to attend and listen to classroom lessons, meaning these children miss the important information they need to learn and participate. Even if they can sit well at the beginning of circle time, odds are that by the end, a few children will be lying on the floor, will be sitting against a wall, will have climbed into a teacher's lap, or will have repositioned their hips into a W-sit position.

After children leave the floor and transition to a group table or desk, sometimes the size of their chair or the height of a table is not appropriate for them. Feet might be dangling in the air. Tables are sometimes so high that children have to lean forward onto the table to reach things. Adults often remind children to sit up, but that's hard for them to do when the tables or chairs just aren't the right sizes for their bodies. Instead, offer chairs and tables that are appropriately sized for the children who use them.

In a classroom setting, keep in mind some simple rules regarding body positioning to help children achieve the best posture so they can focus on their learning.

On the floor or the ground, a ring sit with the legs crossed is often preferred for activities such as circle time. Ideally, when a child is sitting in a chair, their feet should be flat on the floor, with their hips, knees, and ankles forming a 90-degree angle. This is often referred to as the 90-90-90 rule. The top of the table or desk should be about two inches above their elbow.

Along with the improvement in children's focus, making sure playrooms and classrooms have the right-sized tables and chairs for children's ages can make a big difference in their performance while using fine motor skills. Optimal positioning allows for better control in the hands.

Case Study: Encouraging a Child to Sit during Circle Time

At the beginning of circle time, Benito is in a W-sit position. Halfway through the book you're reading, you notice he is lying on the floor and rolling around. How can you redirect his sitting posture to help him be more attentive?

Benito's behavior might indicate that his trunk is weak. If you have alternative seating, such as a cube chair, a preschool chair, or an air-filled cushion, that might help Benito sit without getting too tired. Having him sit against a nearby wall (if it's adjacent to the circle-time area) might also provide stability. Either option can give Benito the support he needs to stay within the boundaries of appropriate sitting for circle time.

Standard Classroom Seating Options

Often, teachers are limited to the furniture they are given or find in their classroom. If the furniture is not the right size to accommodate the children, here are some suggestions to try. First, check to see if either the table or chairs are adjustable in height. If so, a team member might have to use tools to adjust the size. When considering room arrangement, you might group children by their size and adjust the heights of the furniture accordingly. Many teachers like their classrooms to look uniform, but it is more important to accommodate the children appropriately.

If the chairs and desks are too high and are not adjustable, you can still help children achieve better positioning. Placing a step stool under each child's feet can help. Don't have step stools? Try stacked reams of copy paper or sturdy boxes. Do you have a friend or family member who is handy and likes to build? You may be able to find someone who can build some footrests for your classroom.

It's also important to teach children about proper sitting posture so they can self-correct. I've often heard teachers or therapists tell children, "Feet flat. Bottoms back!" Reminding children of this frequently, even in the middle of an activity, helps bring awareness to their sitting posture.

Flexible Seating Options

There are lots of flexible seating options for use in a classroom or at home if the existing equipment is not ideal. These types of chairs, or *dynamic seating systems*, often help support positioning in children who might have poor strength, extra energy, sensory issues, or a diagnosis such as autism or ADHD.

It's important that children have a supportive chair to sit in at times throughout the day. As discussed earlier, a child with poor posture and trunk weakness will not be able to demonstrate as much fine motor control and coordination without a supportive position to work in. Having proper seating ultimately aids in improving coordination, which in turn leads to accuracy and overall improved quality of their performance. The following are some great seating options for a home or a classroom.

Stacking Chairs

These sturdy chairs have back support and armrests and are low to the ground so they won't tip over, making them an excellent choice for young children to sit in.

Cube Chairs

In a preschool setting, cube chairs are popular. This is a sturdy plastic chair that allows children a few different sitting options. It's useful for children who have poor core strength and need additional support, and it works well to redirect those who like to W-sit. Flip this chair up onto the flat side and it will also hold the weight of an adult.

Wobble Stools

Not only are wobble stools good for children who like to move while they learn—because children have to shift their balance forward and backward as well as side to side to stay upright—these seats are also a good way to help children build core strength. Note that working on unstable surfaces like wobble stools can lead to fatigue for those who lack endurance, so have regular, sturdy chairs nearby to transition to.

Therapy-Ball Chairs or Jellyfish Seating

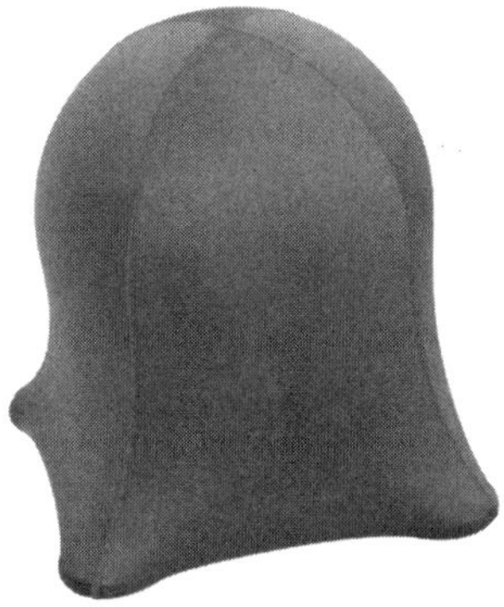

A therapy-ball chair consists of an air-filled exercise ball resting in a sturdy frame. When a child sits on the chair, air from the ball gives input to the spine, and as long as the child's feet are flat on the floor, the seating promotes a more upright posture. Children will want to bounce on these chairs, so make sure to set limits from the beginning. Allow them to bounce a few times at first, so they can get the excitement out of the way and give their bodies some proprioceptive awareness. Then, teach the children how to sit safely when working.

Seat Cushions

Seat cushions are small, air-filled or foam cushions that can be placed on any flat chair or on the floor. Sometimes, just getting a little lift under their bottom with a cushion like this can help children maintain a ring-sit position on the floor with their legs crisscrossed.

Alternative Positions to Sitting

If you do not have access to flexible seating, look around the classroom for step stools and maybe even keep a few regular classroom chairs nearby. If there is a wall or bookcase near your instructional area, position the children who have a harder time sitting up on the floor in front of the wall or near the bookcase for support. If needed, place step stools against the wall to help children sit upright with support. Giving them some posterior support with the wall behind them is almost like sitting in a chair, and it may allow them to sit up for longer periods with more focus.

To help children build more strength, allow them to lie on their stomachs during circle time. This is a good way for children to build trunk extension while also bearing weight through their elbows and forearms to increase upper-body strength. The use of co-contraction, meaning the muscles around the shoulder joint contract at the same time, will build strength and endurance.

Try not to penalize children or get frustrated with them for any nontraditional sitting postures. Generally, there is either a muscle-strength or sensory reason why they aren't sitting upright with good posture for a length of time. A nonpreferred position should be a cue that you need to be flexible and try something different. Be open-minded, and try to use any available tools to accommodate their posture. Allowing for more support through the use of a chair is a better option than sitting on the rug in an uncomfortable position. To immediately improve their posture so they can be ready to engage, help them reposition their body, or offer a chair or cushion to sit. Finding a way for a child to demonstrate a good sitting posture, even if they need flexible seating, will help them engage and attend to fine motor learning opportunities more easily.

★ ★ ★

Now that you understand more about how children develop their core and upper-body strength, how that connects to their fine motor skills, and how you can help them develop core and upper-body muscles through fun activities and exercises, we turn our attention to specific supports for fine motor skills. In chapter 3, we learn all about how to help those little hands to do awesome activities accurately.

CHAPTER 3: Hand Skill Development

In this chapter, you'll learn about children's amazing tiny hands. You'll discover how young children's hands and fine motor skills develop and will learn the types of grasp patterns children use for fine motor–related activities. How children use these skills, called *visual motor skills*, to perform a specific activity are discussed in greater detail in later chapters.

The Progression of Fine Motor Skill Development

Fine motor skills improve and show more refinement and coordination over time. After a baby is born, they use reflexive, uncontrolled movements that lead to larger but still uncoordinated movements. Then, as children develop into the toddler, preschool, and elementary age ranges, their actions become more complex, controlled, and refined.

- A baby will reach for a rattle, hold it with their entire fist or palm, and bring it to their mouth to explore it with their tongue.
- A toddler will pick up a puzzle piece of a table with their whole hand, turn the piece around, look at it, scan the board for the match, then use either one or both hands to place it into the matching location. A child will complete this series of actions as many times as needed until the puzzle is finished.

- A preschool-aged child will pick up a marker, hold it with one hand while pulling off the cap with the other, and then use the marker to draw a person, complete with a head, facial features, body, arms, legs, fingers, and toes.
- A school-aged child will use two hands at the same time to complete the complicated steps of tying their shoes, forming bows that stay secure.

Similar to the developmental milestones in chapter 1, children's developing hand skills and grasp patterns also follow a general timeline. Note that, while children develop fine motor skills, they are also developing their core muscle strength, vision, cognition, and social-emotional skills. The stage of development of these other skills will have a direct effect on whether a child can hit the milestones for grasp development.

Let's take a look at the structure of a child's hand for reference.

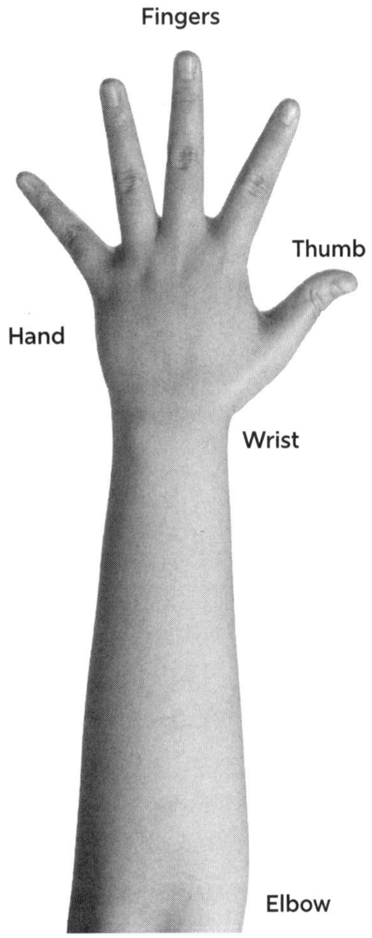

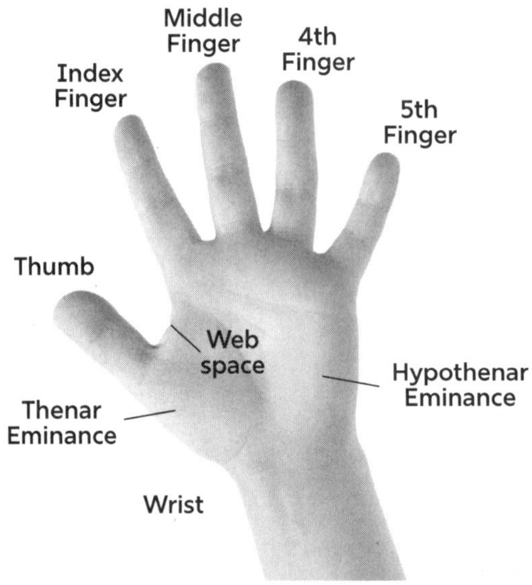

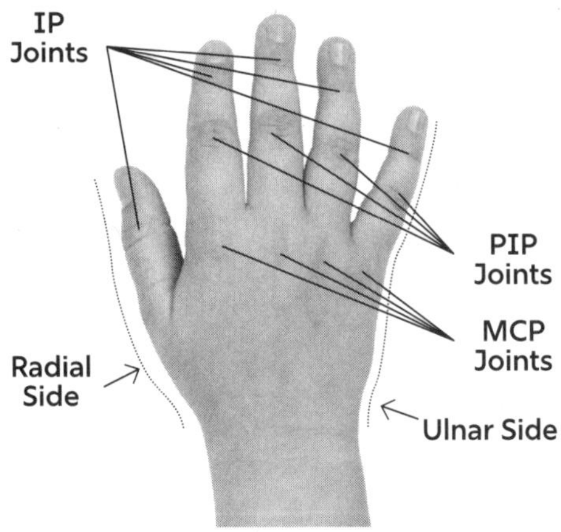

Thumb, index finger, middle finger, 4th finger, 5th finger

Web space (that's the curvature between the thumb and index finger)

Wrist

MCP joints (that's the knuckles where finger and thumb meet hand)

PIP joints (that's the middle finger joints)

IP joint (that's the tip joint of each finger and thumb)

Thenar eminence (that's the fat pad at base of thumb)

Hypothenar eminence (that's the fat pad on pinky side of hand)

Radial side (that's the thumb side of the hand)

Ulnar side (that's the pinky side of the hand)

Grasp Patterns and Hand Development

The hand has two major functions when it comes to grasp patterns: power and precision.

A *power grasp* is when all the fingers are needed at the same time, such as when holding a toothbrush, picking up a water bottle, or drinking out of a glass.

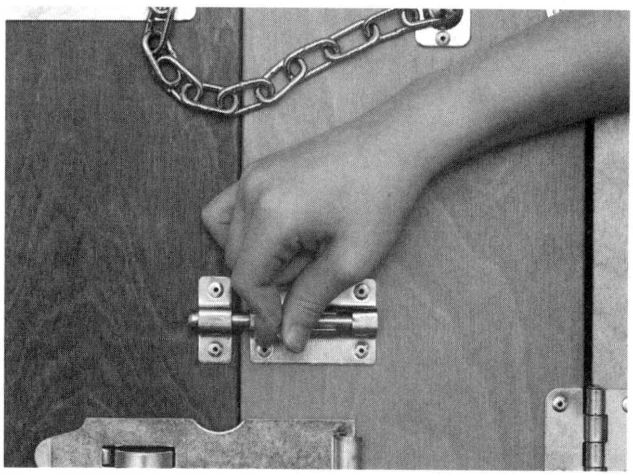

Precision grasps are needed to do more-skilled activities. Precision grasps use the thumb and index finger, or the thumb, index, and middle finger, to hold a pen, pick up small beads, or twist the cap off a toothpaste tube. The ability to demonstrate *positive separation of the hand* (Case-Smith and O'Brien, 2015), or to switch between a power and precision grasp pattern, fully develops around the age of four.

When babies are born, their hands are often fisted while they are awake, but when they are asleep, the fingers are relaxed. A baby is born with *reflexes*, involuntary motions that are triggered by certain actions. When you place a finger inside the palm of a baby, for example, they will automatically squeeze your finger firmly; this is known as the *palmar grasp reflex*. (Lots of people mistake this for an indication of the baby's strength.) As a child develops, this reaction becomes less intense and *integrates*, which means it disappears over time as the baby gains more active control of their hands. But a palmar grasp reflex is an important step in grasp development. In just a few months' time, it will help babies learn to pick up and let go of their toys when playing.

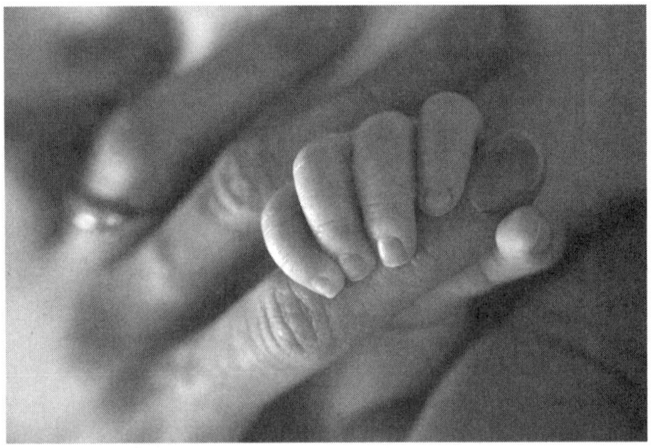

At three months of age, when a baby is lying on their back and their head is in alignment with their body, they will bring their hands together at their stomach, using one hand to explore the other. This symmetrical use of their hands at the *midline*, or the imaginary vertical line at the center of the body, is another important step in fine motor skill development. This action is one of the first steps of *bilateral coordination*, which is the ability to use both hands at the same time to hold items.

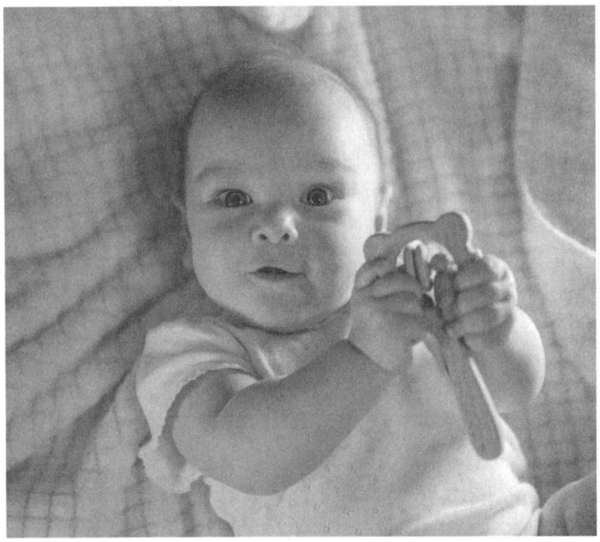

At around four to five months of age, babies can purposefully use their arms to reach out for items such as rattles, teethers, and large toys. They use a palmar grasp to pick up and hold the desired item while exploring it with their mouth and senses. During this stage of development, the palmar grasp reflex is still integrating, so it initially helps babies to keep toys positioned in the palm of the hand. At this age, however, babies do not have active control of their thumbs and often keep them positioned next to their index fingers. While babies continue to develop their upper-body strength through tummy time, their ability to reach out with one hand independently of the other emerges.

Showing more fine motor control at around six to seven months, babies begin using their hands to reach for and grasp moving items. Babies can also sit up on their own and use their hands to play with toys without losing their balance. In this stage, you might notice a baby holding a toy such as a rattle or large block and easily passing it from one hand to the other. Babies at this age enjoy cause-and-effect play, as they can easily push buttons to activate lights and sounds on simple toys.

Bilateral coordination continues to develop as children hold or stabilize a toy in one hand while the other hand is able to spin, flick, crinkle, pull, and manipulate other sensory features of a toy.

At seven months, babies can hold one toy in each hand. Around eight months, they like to do this and bang the toys on a table or bang them together. Around this age, families also start to offer finger foods, such as small pieces of cereal placed on the child's high-chair tray. A baby will attempt to pick up these small food items with a *raking grasp pattern*, which is using their ring and pinky fingers along with the flat part of their hand opposite their thumb on the surface. They scoop the food into their palm, then bring their hand to their mouth and lick or eat the food out of their palm.

Families and caregivers may see babies use a *radial digital grasp pattern* around eight to nine months of age. For example, as a baby picks up a block using their fingers, they use their thumb to move it away from the palm and hold the block with the thumb and

the index and middle fingers. There is now a visible space between the toy and the palm of their hand.

Around eight to ten months of age, a baby is also developing the ability to pick up very small pieces of soft finger foods with more precision, using just the tips of their thumb and index finger, while their other fingers are curled into the palm. This is called a *pincer grasp*, and it allows children to be precise and controlled. Later on, this skill will serve

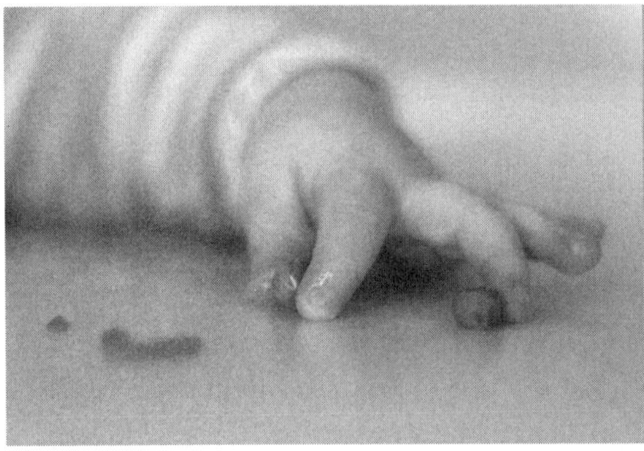

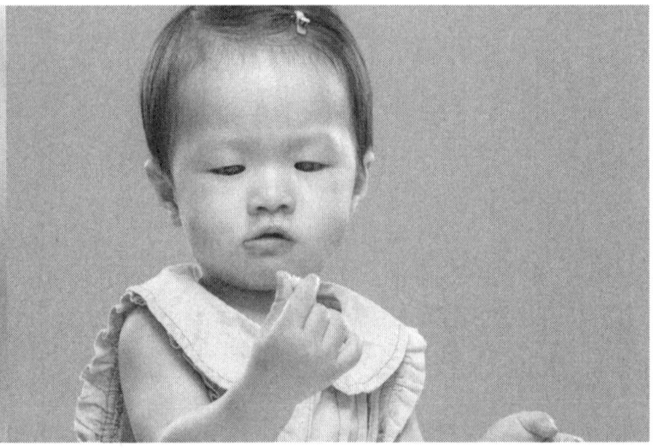

them well for more complicated activities, such as ripping paper, picking up coins to be placed into a piggy bank, pulling a zipper up and down a track on a coat, or manipulating small buttons on a shirt. Buttoning is a common skill that many children lack, and it can frustrate them in an early childhood setting. A *key pinch grasp pattern*, also known as a *lateral grip*, generally develops before a pincer grasp between eight and ten months of age, but it differs from a pincer grasp. Instead of the thumb touching the tip of the index finger, it touches the side of the index finger. This grasp pattern is often used during fine motor activities, such as stringing beads, or when completing household activities such as inserting a key into a lock and then using strength to turn the item from one side to another.

One-year-olds are learning to pick up a crayon and scribble on paper with a *pronated grasp pattern*. This is when the whole hand grasps a crayon and the child makes marks on the paper by rotating their entire hand so that the thumb is closest to the paper. It is a common grasp pattern that many children don't advance from as they get older. If a child continues to use it, especially around age three and older, they will require support and intervention to change their grasp pattern.

Release Patterns and Bilateral Coordination

Now that we've covered grasp patterns—or how children pick items up—let's take a closer look at the next step: how young children develop the ability to let go of items (called *release patterns*) and to let them go with accuracy and control (called *bilateral coordination*).

Release patterns begin around six months of age as a baby learns to transfer toys from one hand to the other. They also work to pick up food off the tray and release it into their mouth, but in the beginning it's not always a smooth release. At first, the baby has to use their other hand or their lips to begin to let the item go with control.

Around ten months of age, controlled, purposeful release patterns develop when a baby starts intentionally flinging items out of their hand, or when they learn how fun it is to drop food off the edge of their high chair onto the floor.

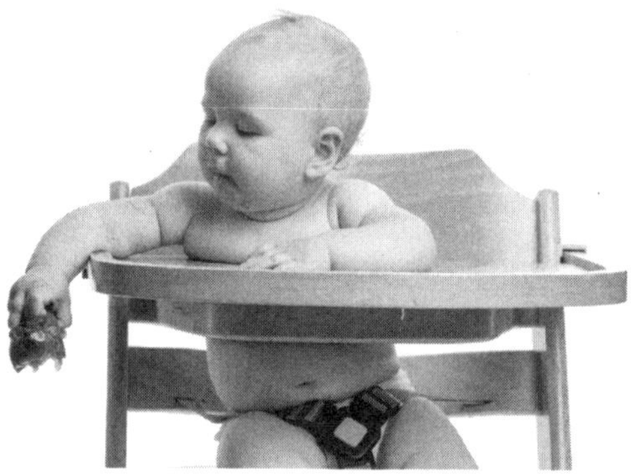

At this age, babies learn how to play with shape sorters. If a piece is already positioned in the correct hole, a baby will push the piece in with their fingers. For shape sorters that have larger openings, a baby will often lift a piece to the correct hole and then rest their palm on the edge of that hole. This action helps to encourage the fingers to extend, ultimately letting the child release the toy and drop it into the container. The action will happen randomly at first, then in a more controlled and purposeful way.

Around one year of age, children can use their hands for more functions. When a child holds an object in a radial digital grasp pattern, their release patterns begin to develop more control. For example, the child now has the skills to stack one block on top of another without the second block immediately falling off. A one-year-old can grasp a sippy-cup handle and bring the cup to their mouth to drink. Many children of this age enjoy repeatedly putting items into and taking them out of containers for dump-and-fill play. Some are able to complete simple puzzles with large handles and can use a pincer-grasp pattern to pick up small food items and drop them into a container with a small opening.

Two-year-olds can use release patterns and bilateral coordination with even greater accuracy. In imaginative play, one child might hold a doll while another child feeds it with a bottle. They might push and drive cars along a track, and twist and manipulate buttons and levers on pop-up toys. At this age, many children pick up and hold utensils to scoop and pierce foods when eating. Two-year-olds also love turning the pages of a book. They can take off their socks and shoes, learn to imitate some block designs, and begin to string large beads.

What about Handedness?

Many families and teachers have lots of questions about *handedness*, which is when a child shows a preference for and ultimately the consistent use of the same hand for skilled activities, such as drawing. At younger ages, and not until a child enters the school-aged years, handedness is generally not much of a concern. It's important to develop the skills in each hand equally.

It's actually more concerning in the toddler years to see a child with a strong hand preference or dominance. For children who specialize too early, their other hand still has a job to do to stabilize or hold and support containers, other toys, and so on. Basic levels of strength and coordination are needed, even for the "helper hand," or the nondominant hand. For children who specialize too early, this could lead to inconsistent skills and a lot of frustration.

Handedness becomes important in the school years, when children begin to do activities such as cutting with scissors, coloring, and writing letters and numbers. Having a dominant hand with well-developed skills makes it easier to perform activities with precision and speed. However, children are often referred to an OT when they have not yet developed a hand preference by kindergarten or when they frequently switch toys from one hand to the other while playing. At some point, this repeated switching of toys, pencils, and other items from one hand to the other is just not efficient and takes a lot of extra time. Many teachers and family members look for feedback on which hand they should help promote, so therapists look at the differences in the child's skills from one hand to the other to provide more information.

Some children will be clearly right- or left-hand dominant. Others might have "unestablished handedness," which means they might also have "mixed handedness" and swap toys and items from one hand to another. This can be common at the preschool level and should not be confused with being *ambidextrous* (having the ability to use both hands equally with the same amount of well-developed skill).

While it's not as common as it used to be, some children are "switched handers," which means they might have been prone to being left-handed but have been taught to complete skills such as writing and drawing with the right hand. This is common in certain cultures that promote right-handedness.

A much larger percentage of the population is right-handed than is left-handed. It is estimated that about 10 percent of the population in general is left-handed (Corey, Hurley, and Foundas, 2001). Males are 25 percent more likely to be left-handed than females are (Henderson and Pehoski, 2006). There can be a genetic aspect to handedness as well. If a parent is left-handed, there is a higher likelihood their child will be left-handed.

Left-handers tend to switch hands depending upon the task and will frequently use the right hand for some tasks. Right-handers generally use just the right hand for all tasks and use the left hand to support toys or stabilize paper while writing or drawing.

Handedness is also correlated to the development of brain structures (Sha et al., 2021). Around two years of age, when children can stabilize an item with one hand and use the other to perform a skill, a hand preference begins to emerge. By the age of four and a half, most children are showing a dominant hand; true dominance may not be fully established until between the ages of six and nine.

Here's the challenging part: Preschool-aged children are now asked to complete highly complicated fine motor tasks for writing at younger ages, when hand dominance might not yet even be expected. Poor hand strength can lead to hand switching. When one hand gets tired or fatigued, children will switch to the opposite hand to continue and finish a task. So, it's also important to identify whether poor strength might be affecting a child's handedness.

As a Teacher, Should I Make Them Choose a Hand?

If a child is nearing kindergarten age and not showing hand dominance, you might need to watch them more closely to get more information. Sometimes, children who do not have a solid dominance will just reach for the toy that's closest to their hand. If toys are scattered all over a table, toys on the right side will be picked up with the right hand, while toys on the left side will get picked up with the left hand. Many children are not able to cross midline, which is reaching smoothly from one side of their body to the opposite side. For a child who has not developed the ability to cross midline, you might notice them transferring items into their other hand at the center of their body.

If you aren't sure which hand is dominant for a child, try offering them markers, scissors, and toys at the midline. This means when the child is sitting down at a table, place the item directly on the table in front of them at the center of their body. Ask them to pick up the tool. Which hand do they naturally reach out with? Try it again—is it consistent? You might begin to see that the child does have a preference developing. Children who are not crossing midline will often pick up items with their nonpreferred hand and transfer them into the other hand at midline. They might not naturally reach across the body to pick up manipulatives with their preferred hand.

Still not sure? Watch the child play. Give them manipulatives such as blocks, pegs, and playdough, and see if they tend to use one hand to do more work than the other. If they are putting blocks into a container, which hand is holding the container? This is the stabilizing hand, which is generally not the dominant hand. Do they complete the activity from start to finish without switching from one hand to another? This is most likely their preferred hand, which will become dominant. From one activity to another, is the child always choosing the same hand? This can also indicate dominance.

If you still aren't sure, keep watching. Even if the child uses both hands, do they demonstrate better control, accuracy, attention to tasks, and performance when using one hand versus the other? Are the grasp patterns more developmentally advanced for one hand versus the other?

While we need both hands to develop a basic level of function before one hand becomes more specialized, it's important to give children ample time to develop before they are influenced or forced to pick one hand over the other. If they are at the kindergarten level, when more writing is required, then you might have to use your observations of their performance to help promote a hand dominance.

The "Helper Hand"

An important element of fine motor skills involves being able to use two hands at the same time. The nondominant hand becomes the *stabilizing hand*, or the "helper hand." This is the one that supports a cup, bowl, plate, paper, toy, or other object while the dominant hand performs a more complicated action.

Part of bilateral coordination is stabilizing a piece of paper during school activities. Many children do not naturally hold the paper with the nondominant hand, so the paper will slide around the table. Even though the stabilizing hand doesn't do all the action, it plays an important part in the successful completion of these activities, and its use should be encouraged. Some children need lots of reminders to use their "helper hand." A fun strategy that is part of the Learning Without Tears writing curriculum is to have children name their helper hands. Then, if "Stanley" isn't doing his job, the teacher can remind "Stanley" how to be a good helper and hold the paper while the child is writing.

In-Hand Manipulation Skills

After children learn how to pick up and let go of items using an accurate release, over time they will demonstrate more speed, accuracy, and coordination as they manipulate and engage with smaller toys. Development of these complicated in-hand manipulation skills is helpful in developing a more refined grasp pattern, which is needed to hold pencils and utensils.

In-hand manipulation is when children pick up and maneuver toys in a variety of ways before they accurately release them or complete an intricate activity. These activities are important to promote through play. One in-hand manipulation skill called *translation* involves picking up small toys or food items and maneuvering them from the palm to the fingers for placement. Activities using this skill include picking up a coin off a table, then moving it to the fingers for placement in a piggy bank. Other translation activities include picking up and pushing small pegs into playdough and picking up and moving snacks from the palm to the fingertips for finger feeding.

Shift is another in-hand manipulation skill that requires the use of the fingertips to move something, such as a pencil, forward and backward. This skill is used by elementary school-aged children who pick up a pencil by the middle or end of the shaft and need to inch their fingers down closer to the tip. It's also observed when someone reaches up to the corner of a book and separates the pages to turn them.

Simple rotation includes being able to roll items in the fingertips. *Complex rotation* is the ability to hold a small item and rotate it around in the fingertips at least 180 degrees.

Rotation is involved when trying to make small balls with dough using the fingertips. It's also observed when rotating a puzzle piece for placement or handling construction-toy pieces such as Legos.

The *intrinsic muscles* are the small muscles inside the palm of the hand that help children to complete dynamic hand motions, such as moving the fingertips back and forth when coloring and when writing in small spaces. Strength in these muscles is important to reduce fatigue while completing precise actions. When coloring, children can hold a pencil, marker, or crayon and make linear and circular motions that allow them to accurately color within small, defined areas for a time without the hand getting tired.

As mentioned earlier in this chapter, positive separation of the hand is when a child can use their thumb, index, and middle finger to perform a skill, while their fourth and fifth fingers are flexed or tucked into the palm. Using this skill shows that the child has developed the power grasp and precision grasp and can use them according to the activity that needs to be completed.

★ ★ ★

Next, we'll look at the types of grasp patterns, organized by chronological age, that are used when coloring, drawing, and writing. We'll also explore how you can support young children in developing these skills for school readiness.

CHAPTER 4:
Grasp Development for School Readiness

In this chapter, we review the different grasp patterns introduced in the previous chapter, look at how children of different ages use the patterns in school-readiness activities, and learn strategies to build children's hand and pinch strength. The rest of the chapter describes how you can support children's grasp development by teaching them how to hold a writing tool and how to use different types of crayons, markers, and pencil grips.

As I'm sure you are already learning, OTs use many fancy technical names to describe how a child uses their hands when playing. It can all be overwhelming, but you don't need to memorize all these terms. Instead, take some time to look at the photos of the different grasp patterns, and try to match the grasp patterns you see to what you should expect to see given the ages of the children in your classroom setting. That way, if you expect to see a higher-level grasp pattern because you teach kindergarten, yet a child is using a less refined or more immature grasp pattern, such as one that you might expect of a two-year-old, you can spot it and quickly offer some strategies to develop the grasp pattern further. And in case you are wondering how, don't worry—I've got lots of ideas included here to help you.

Grasp Patterns by Chronological Order

A *palmar grasp* is when the whole fist supports the tool with the thumb straight up in the air and the writing tool emerges from the hand by the fifth finger. This is often seen in children ages one to one and a half.

Two-to-three-year-olds transition to a *pronated grasp pattern* or *digital pronate grasp*. This is when the whole hand grasps a marker, pair of scissors, or a utensil. But, unlike in the palmar grasp pattern, the forearm is now rotated or turned so that the thumb is pointing down toward the paper. At certain ages this is developmentally appropriate, but if this grasp pattern is still present as children get into preschool and the early elementary years, it is considered immature. This grasp could be problematic as children are trying to write complicated alphabet letters, because it does not offer the control and skill children need for these tasks. It often requires remediation and intervention.

Young children also use *fingertip grasp patterns* with small toys and foods. This is when you observe a young child using all four fingers and their thumb to hold and manipulate an item. There are different variations of fingertip grasp patterns. For our purposes, we will talk about these grasp patterns as they relate to holding writing utensils such as crayons, markers, and pencils:

- ***Quadripod grasp pattern* (three to four years old):** This grasp pattern is when the writing utensil is mainly supported with the thumb, index, middle, and ring fingers. While it is not considered the most mature grasp pattern, for many children it is still a good one to get the job done successfully. If a child in preschool exhibits this grasp pattern, it is still important to continue to promote the most mature grasp pattern. In the following pictures, you'll see a C-shaped web space (the curvature between the

thumb and the index finger), which demonstrates appropriate intrinsic hand strength so the fingers can move during writing, coloring, and drawing.

- ***Static tripod grasp pattern*** **(three and a half to four years old):** In this grasp pattern, the thumb, index, and middle fingers support the writing utensil. Movement when writing does not come from the fingers; the movement comes from the elbow, while the hand remains rigid.

- ***Dynamic tripod grasp pattern*** **(four to seven years old):** This grasp pattern is the most mature one. The pencil rests in the web space, at the joint of the index finger, and the fingertips rest on the edge of the writing utensil. The difference with this grasp pattern is that the forearm, wrist, and hand are stable on the writing surface. During writing and coloring, the fingers move up, down, back, and forth, to get within small areas successfully with control. A C-shaped web space can be observed, demonstrating appropriate intrinsic hand strength. This grasp pattern is often observed around the age of five.

- ***Adaptive tripod grasp pattern*:** This is also considered a mature grasp pattern, but the pencil rests in between the index and middle fingers rather than in the web space. The index finger, middle finger, and thumb still support the tip of the pencil and move when writing; the pencil is just in a more stable position between the two fingers. A C-shaped web space can be observed, demonstrating appropriate intrinsic hand strength. This is a very stable grasp pattern but is one that generally requires an occupational therapist or teacher to suggest. Not many children consider using it, but many like it once it's demonstrated.

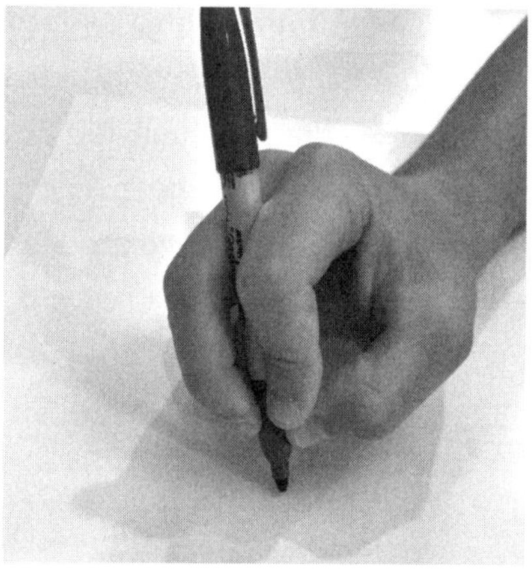

Immature Grasp Patterns That Require Support

The following grasp patterns can be ineffective and show that there are some strength and coordination skill deficits. These grasp patterns will need intervention to fix them; I've included some specific activities to try to build the strength and coordination needed to get to the more mature grasp patterns. In many cases, making a simple substitution in a routine, such as using glue bottles instead of glue sticks, can build in more opportunities for practice and repetition.

- ***Lateral (or thumb-wrap) grasp pattern*:** This grasp is characterized by the thumb resting against the index finger, with a closed web space. Using tweezers, tongs, and hand-strengthening activities discussed later in this chapter will help to build intrinsic muscle strength for a well-developed web space.
- ***Lateral quadripod (or thumb-wrap) grasp pattern*:** This grasp also demonstrates a closed web space with the thumb wrapped around the shaft of the writing utensil, while the index, middle, and ring fingers support the utensil. This causes the wrist to flex inward, making writing a challenge. Thumb-wrap grasp patterns can lead to fatigue when writing. For flexed wrists, using easels to build strength is an excellent way to redirect the grasp pattern. When the wrist is extended while using the easel, this position eliminates the awkward wrist position.

- ***Multifinger grasp pattern*:** This is a grasp pattern that uses the thumb and four fingers. Often, the index finger is positioned in the middle of the writing utensil and curled around it near the top. This is an inefficient grasp pattern that often leads to pain over time due to stress on the joint.

If immature grasp patterns are present, they may require intervention. Children with these grasp patterns may have deficits in certain skills, generally in strength and coordination, that can be improved to transition to a more refined grasp pattern. In the next section, we look at ways to build hand and pinch strength.

Building Hand and Pinch Strength

Hand strength is key. Building the small intrinsic muscles in the hand helps in developing proper grasp patterns for writing and cutting. It also helps develop the endurance needed when completing these activities for longer periods. The ability to use the thumb, index, and middle fingers independently from the other fingers—known as positive separation of the hand—is important too. This section provides activities you can do in your classroom or send home with families to help children develop these abilities.

Building Whole-Hand Strength

- Here are some ways to build overall hand strength. This first involves a *power grasp* using all five fingers at the same time.
- Use sensory mediums that offer some kind of resistance or, even better, varying levels of resistance. Encourage children to squeeze, pull, roll, and mix compounds with one hand or two hands at the same time.
    - Try compounds such as playdough, putty, and modeling clay, such as Crayola Model Magic, Crazy Aaron's Thinking Putty, Butter Cloudz, or TheraPutty. TheraPutty comes in multiple colors, and each color represents a different level of resistance. Be sure to monitor children's use of TheraPutty, because it will expand and cause a mess that cannot be removed from carpets or clothing.
    - For additional strength-building options, add extruders such as a cookie press and garlic presses to the playdough area.
- Provide fidgets and stress balls that have different textures inside them. The fidget or stress ball should fit inside the palm of the child's hand so they are squeezing with all five fingers. The child can also roll and push down on the top of a stress ball with their palm. Aim to complete these activities for ten repetitions. Pushing, pulling, twisting and squeezing for a specific duration of time or a certain number of repetitions can

also build strength. Many children who have poor hand strength also lack endurance and will either get frustrated quickly or try to avoid these tasks altogether. Using a timer or counting along with them can help children participate for a short duration of time; then allow them to rest. Here are some fidgets and stress balls to try:

- NeeDoh Nice Cubes
- Slow-rising squish toys
- Ball-popper toys (the kind that children can squeeze to push a ball out of the toy's mouth)
- Stress balls (both squishy and stretchy varieties)

- Offer children filled water bottles with squeeze triggers to water plants, erase chalk drawings on pavement, and clean toys.
- Add sponges, cylinders, and bulb syringes to the water table, and encourage children to wring or squeeze water from these objects into a container and measure it.
- Create a Mr. Mouth. Carefully use a pair of scissors to cut a slit in a tennis ball. Show children how to use their thumb and whole hand to squeeze the tennis ball open while the other hand inserts coins, pegs, and small toys into the "mouth."
- Provide families with the list of squeeze tools recommended in chapter 6, such as tea-bag infusers, resistive tongs, strawberry hullers, and mini squeeze bottles, which are easy to use at home.
- Instead of using glue sticks, consider using glue bottles that require squeezing.
- Encourage children to pull apart large magnetic toys with their fingertips.

Building Fingertip Strength

Building strength with the grasp patterns noted below will help to develop coordination and strength for the precision side of the hand. Incorporating classroom and at-home play activities with toys that encourage these hand positions can, over time, have a positive effect on how accurately children write, color, hold their utensils, and play games.

Index-Finger Isolation

Extending the index finger in a pointing fashion while closing the other fingers into the palm is known as *index-finger isolation*. Children generally make this gesture when they are pointing to items they want or sharing their excitement about something happening around them. Some children are not able to easily imitate this hand position and might just gesture with an open hand.

To promote index-finger isolation, encourage tracing activities such as the following:

- Making letters in shaving cream or other sensory mediums
- Poking playdough
- Tapping, pointing, swiping, and dragging icons with the index finger rather than the thumb when engaging with apps on a tablet or smartphone

Tip Pinch

A *tip pinch* is when the thumb and index finger meet at the tips and the remaining fingers are flexed into the palm. Strength with this grasp pattern is important for pulling apart small snaps or beads and for manipulating buttons on a shirt.

Three-Jaw Chuck

A *three-jaw chuck grasp pattern* is when the thumb, index finger, and middle finger approach an item, such as a clothespin, and squeeze it with the index and middle fingers on the top and the thumb on the bottom. The ring and pinky fingers stay flexed into the palm.

The following activities and toys can help children work on a three-jaw chuck hand position to build strength:

- **Activities**
    - Pick up a clothespin in a three-jaw chuck grasp pattern. Open and close the clothespin slowly ten times, then take a break.
    - Use clothespins to pick up pompom balls. Clothespins are available in different resistances that range from 1–5 pounds.
    - Pick up and pinch golf tees with a three-jaw-chuck grasp pattern, then insert them into a small piece of a pool noodle.
- **Toys**
    - Snapo blocks
    - Snap cubes
    - Mini pop beads

- Spinning tops
- Windup toys
- Squigz suction cups
- Mr. Potato Head
- Spring-loaded pop-up toys (generally found in party-supply aisles and prize bins)
- Pop-tubes
- Mini pegboards

Squigz

Squigz are toys that have different-sized suction cups. These toys can build children's hand strength and bilateral control as they stick them together and pull them apart.

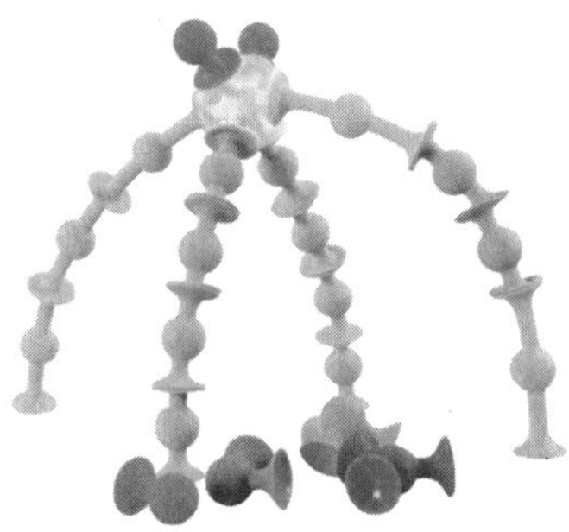

- **Make it easier:** Attach the suction cups to a table, and have children remove them by grasping them and pulling them off the table.
- **Make it harder:** Attach several suction cups together to create a design or person. Stick the creation to a vertical surface, such as a door, so that a child has to extend their wrist and then pull to detach the pieces. This requires more coordination than detaching the toys from a horizontal surface such as a tabletop.

Using Sensory Mediums to Build Pinch Strength

Sensory mediums, such as playdough, Kinetic Sand, TheraPutty, slime, and Playfoam, help build hand strength and can also build pinch strength when used with different tools.

- Add tools, such as extruders, stamps, molds, cookie cutters, toy body parts (such as arms, legs, eyes, noses, and mouth), and small pegs, with playdough to help children build pinch strength.
- Use stamps and molds with Kinetic Sand.

- Offer children small pegs and coins to use with TheraPutty. Be sure to monitor children's use of TheraPutty because it will expand and cause a mess that cannot be removed from carpet or clothing.
- Create your own slime kits, and encourage children to mix in sprinkles, glitter, and scents to build personalized slime.
- Have children roll and shape Playfoam and then place it on letter cards to form the shapes of the letters.

The remainder of this chapter looks at how you can help children develop mature grasp patterns and fine motor skills by teaching them how to hold a writing tool. You can use different types of crayons, markers, and pencil grips, depending on each child's developmental age, to achieve this goal.

Holding a Writing Tool

Some children will just pick up a writing tool and get to work, but it's always important to teach young children how to hold their writing tools. This is especially true if children are learning about ways to pick up their utensils. A teacher or family member can cue them to fix their grasp as needed, and children will learn to reposition objects on their own without help until this habit becomes ingrained. To make this easier, make the process fun!

Animal Fingers

Model keeping your ring and pinky fingers flexed or tucked into the palm, with the thumb, index, and middle fingers remaining out. Ask the child their favorite animal, then open and close your thumb and index and middle fingers as if they're an animal's mouth. You might be quacking like a duck, roaring like a dinosaur, barking like a dog, or meowing like a cat; find an animal the child is motivated by. Model how to hold a writing utensil with this grasp. Encourage the child to pick up the tool and place it in the "animal's mouth" to reposition it. Repeat this activity over time until the child eventually learns how to pick up the item on their own.

Pinch and Flip

Hold a marker or crayon and set its tip on a table so the item is standing up straight. If using Crayola-type items that have a squiggle on the wrapper near the tip, encourage the child to pinch the squiggles with their thumb and index finger. Then, tell them to pick up the writing tool and "flip" it back without letting go so that the tool falls onto the C-shaped web space of the child's hand. The tip of the tool will then be pointing toward the child's shoulder.

Using Different Types of Crayons

Lots of classrooms have crayons, and there are different types of crayons for each age group. Here is a suggested progression of crayons for children from infancy to elementary age that can help improve children's grasp patterns.

Don't throw out broken crayons! They are excellent for helping children develop a tripod-style grasp pattern, because the short pieces can only be held by using the thumb and index and middle finger in a tip pinch grasp. Using smaller, broken crayons will help children use a more mature, natural fine motor grasp pattern right from the start.

- **Crayola Washable Palm-Grasp Crayon (12 months and up):** These large, egg-shaped crayons fill the whole hand and allow younger children with a palmar grasp to make marks on a page.
- **Jumbo crayons (12 months and up):** These long, thick, jumbo-size crayons are easy for young toddlers to hold with a palmar grasp pattern.
- **Finger crayons (24 months and up):** Finger crayons have a pointed tip and a hollow, rounded base. The index finger can be inserted into the base for stability, or all fingers can hold the rounded edge, which promotes more of a fingertip grasp pattern. Because of the pointed tip, it's hard to hold these crayons in an immature grasp pattern, so they work well for helping children with pronated grasp patterns to transition to fingertip grasp patterns.
- **Triangular crayons (3 years and up):** A triangular crayon naturally promotes a fingertip grasp pattern.
- **Crayola Twistables:** While the manufacturer recommends these for ages three and up, they are probably best for older elementary students. The crayon is housed in a long plastic case, and the end needs to be twisted to reveal the crayon so a child can use it to color.
- **Classic crayons (4 years and up):** These are traditional-sized crayons and are best for children in the early elementary school ages. Preschool-aged children do better with thicker crayons. However, classic crayons can be broken and used with younger children to promote a fingertip grasp pattern.

Using Different Types of Markers

Markers are a great tool to use. Many children prefer them over crayons, as they do not require as much strength to make marks on paper, and the vibrant colors are rewarding. Pay special attention to whether the markers are washable, and always provide supervision as needed, because even washable markers can stain. In general, shorter, fatter markers are better for younger age groups; longer, skinnier markers can be used by older children who have a more developed grasp pattern. Here is a progression of markers for children from toddlerhood to elementary age that can aid them in the use of more mature grasp patterns.

- **Lakeshore Learning My First Washable Markers (18 months and up):** These rounded markers help to fill the whole hand and are best for younger children just beginning to color.
- **Crayola Washable Tripod Grip Markers (24 months and up):** These thick, triangular-shaped markers help to promote a fingertip grasp pattern.
- **Do-a-Dot Art! Markers (3 years and up):** These patented markers are thick and make nice marks. They can be used for drawing, and lots of children like to use them to make dots on their papers when coloring in defined areas.
- **Crayola Color Wonder Mess-Free Markers (3 years and up):** Markers are lovely, but they can be messy. These markers will only work on special Crayola paper. They don't leave marks on tables, carpets, skin, or walls, making them a good toddler option. They do require a few seconds for the color to appear on the paper, which can be challenging for younger children.
- **Crayola Pip-Squeaks (3 years and up):** The company recommends these markers for ages three and up, but in my experience, they are well suited for older preschool and kindergarten-aged students. Pip-Squeak markers are a good choice in general because of their shorter length, which makes them easier for smaller hands to control.
- **Expo Dry-Erase Markers (3 years and up):** These markers work well for lots of activities with young children, as long as they have supervision. These markers are not washable.
- **Crayola Ultra-Clean Washable Markers, Broad Line (6 years and up):** These are the traditional Crayola markers, which are washable but still best-suited for kindergarten-aged students.

- **Crayola Ultra-Clean Washable Markers, Fine Line (8 years and up):** Because of their thin profile, to use these markers properly without fatigue children need to have well-developed grasp patterns. They are best suited for older elementary school–aged children.

★ ★ ★

In this chapter, we reviewed the important grasp patterns children need to have to play with their toys effectively. The next chapter will focus on visual motor skills, which are the functional and meaningful day-to-day activities that children do when they play. Along with good strength and correct grasp patterns for picking up blocks, beads, and other items, children also need visual motor skills to perform activities with those items—for example, picking up beads and placing them on a string to make a necklace, aligning and stacking towers of blocks, and matching puzzle pieces to the correct locations to finish a form-board puzzle.

CHAPTER 5:
Developing Visual Motor Skills through Play

Visual motor skills is a fancy term for using fine motor control along with eye-hand coordination to perform an activity with the hands. These skills are involved when a child manipulates a toy, marker, scissors, or crayon once they grasp it, such as creating a fortress of magnetic tiles where their dinosaurs can sleep, drawing a self-portrait on a piece of paper, or using a plastic knife to cut apart Velcro fruits and vegetables to make a pretend soup. Visual motor skills are the exciting part of promoting fine motor skills, because children get to have fun while playing, learning, and engaging with their world. These skills are important at all ages but become even more so once children start school. Children need precision and control of their bodies and hand movements so they can develop a strong foundation of academic-readiness skills.

Visual Motor Skills by Chronological Age

Examples of visual motor skills for toddlers include picking up a piece from a shape sorter and placing it into the container, inserting a puzzle piece into a form board, and grasping a crayon and using it to scribble. These skills, in turn, help children learn the skill of picking up a utensil and feeding themselves, such as eating ice cream, yogurt, or applesauce with a spoon.

In the preschool years, visual motor skills expand to include using a crayon to color inside the lines or make interconnecting lines to draw a person. These skills, in turn, help children learn how to pick up a pair of scissors and use them to cut out shapes, such as circles and squares, while turning the paper.

As children advance from the early childhood classroom into kindergarten and their elementary years, these skills include expanding their control and thoroughness to color and draw with more attention to detail. They learn to pick up a pencil and begin to learn the strokes and formations needed to write upper- and lowercase letters, eventually enabling them to write their names, words, or short sentences. Visual motor skills that children use at home and at school might include manipulating fasteners on their clothing, such as small buttons or zippers, and using a fork and knife to cut their food.

In the next section, we focus on the use of specific toys that help young children improve their visual motor skills. In my therapy practice with children, I pride myself on finding fun, practical ways to play, so therapy doesn't feel like work. The moment an activity is boring, too difficult, or not fun, a child will take the first opportunity to stop playing or distract themselves by looking for something more exciting.

When choosing different types of toys that children can select during center time or free play, consider the following options. Not only are these toys generally fun, but they will help young children develop solid foundational skills, too. Toys featured in these categories are listed in order of complexity, from the easiest to use with younger age groups to progressively harder ones to challenge older students.

Toys That Build Visual Motor Skills

Here are some popular types of toys that can be instrumental in building a child's visual motor skills through play, beginning in infancy and progressing through the preschool years. Incorporating these types of toys at young ages will build solid visual motor skills needed for school readiness. While I have a lot of experience working as an occupational therapist, as I mentioned earlier, I am also known as the "ToyQueen." For the last fifteen years, I have personally reviewed, played with, and written about hundreds of new toys, and I have built relationships with many toy manufacturers. Each of the following sections covers a general category of popular children's toys. Within each section are a few specific toys to consider that I personally recommend.

Cause-and-Effect Toys

Visual motor skills begin to develop early on as babies explore. Cause-and-effect toys do something fun and unique—such as pop up, light up, or make sounds—when children push or pull different buttons, flaps, or gadgets. Cause-and-effect play that is developed using fine motor skills promotes improved attention and interaction with the world for learning. Fun examples of cause-and-effect toys for the six-to-nine-month age range are jack-in-the-boxes, spinning domes, activity cubes, and pop-up toys.

It is common for children with disabilities such as autism to have delayed fine motor skills and delayed play skills in general. Even if these toys might be designed for younger children, light-up cause-and-effect toys can help build confidence in older children who have delays. These kinds of toys offer immediate feedback through lights and sounds when the child manipulates the right part of a toy.

Looking to add some cause-and-effect toys to your playroom or classroom? Here are a few examples of my favorites:

- 5-in-1 Activity Center by Kaplan Early Learning
- Activity cubes by VTech
- Glow & Discover Light Bar Toy by Baby Einstein
- Magic Touch Xylophone by Baby Einstein
- Press & Glow Spinner by Bright Starts
- Rock 'n' Roller Piano by Fat Brain Toys
- Tumble Ball Dome by Kaplan Early Learning

Containers for Dump-and-Fill Play

The first skill that babies learn when engaging in container play is to dump by turning over containers. Eventually, they begin to reach into an open container, grasp toys, and remove them one after another. Lots of children enjoy taking wooden blocks from a bin or toys out of a shape sorter with its top removed. Then, once they learn how to remove the toys, they begin to want to put them back inside and take them out all over again. Children ages twelve to twenty-four months enjoy dump-and-fill, or spill-and-fill, play. There are many great toys that children can use. Here are a few of my personal favorites:

- Drop and Go Dump Truck by VTech
- InnyBin by Fat Brain Toys

- Fine Motor Discovery Box by Kaplan Early Learning
- Little People School Bus Toy by Fisher-Price
- Peekaboo Learning Farm by Learning Resources

Stackers

At around thirteen to fifteen months, children advance from pushing buttons to beginning to pick up toys and place them with control, working on more refined release patterns. Stackers are an ideal toy to help children develop the ability to let go of toys with the right force and some accuracy. These types of toys generally have some type of ring in the middle, or they may be cups or boxes that stack on top of one another. Many stacker toys include pieces of different sizes, and eventually children learn to notice the differences and put the pieces in a specific order.

Here are some examples of my favorite stacker toys:

- Rock-a-Stack by Fisher-Price
- SpinAgain by Fat Brain Toys
- Stacking cups
- Tobbles Neo by Fat Brain Toys

There is no need to give a young child all the pieces of a stacker toy at once. Giving them two or three to try at first will help them succeed rather than being overwhelmed with too many options.

Sorters

Once children master the basic concept of putting items into and taking them out of containers, they begin to use their fine motor skills to play with shape sorters. They rotate their hands to place pieces into the correct spots, at first by using trial-and-error problem solving. Sorters are most appropriate for children ages twelve to eighteen months.

The VTech Sort and Discover Drum is a great first choice for a sorter. Children can place the pieces in the right openings, but they won't fall through unless they are actually pushed. This is a fun way to begin to engage children in understanding sorters. They will eventually learn which shape goes where just by playfully pushing in after you position the shape at the right opening.

Sorters with fewer shapes are better for younger children, while those with more shapes are best for older children with more refined fine motor skills and longer attention spans. Children can recognize simple shapes—such as circles, squares, and triangles—first, even if the sorter is more advanced.

To start engaging a child with a sorter, sit down on the floor with the child. Turn the sorter so that the opening for the circle piece is closest to the child. Get their attention by pointing to the opening, then hand them the circle and see if they try to insert it in the correct spot. If not, while they are holding the shape, guide their hand to the top of the opening, see if they release the circle, then fade your physical support away. Praise and excitement for any efforts children make might help motivate them to keep on trying until they get it right.

Here are some of the best shape sorters to try:

- Shapes and Sounds Box by Kaplan Early Learning
- Sort and Discover Drum by VTech
- Wooden shape sorters by Melissa & Doug
- Daisy Shape Sorter by Quercetti
- Plugzy by Fat Brain Toys

Sort and Discover Drum

Following the instructions, children pick up a shape, match it to the right spot on the lid, then rotate their hand to align the shape in the top and push the piece inside the container.

- **Make it easier:** At first, remove the red lid and just encourage the child to pick up the pieces and put them into the container. Later, align the shapes by placing them in the correct locations in the lid and rest them on top so they're ready to be pushed in. Encourage the child to use their finger to push each shape through the lid. Hand them only the circles at first, because that shape doesn't require much wrist rotation to align them.
- **Make it harder:** Hand the child all the pieces of the sorter at the same time, which will require that they sort through the items, match them to the correct locations, then use wrist control to turn the pieces to fit them in the holes before inserting them.

Puzzles

Puzzles are a popular visual motor skill activity that is first offered to children around one year of age. Many puzzles have thick wooden handles on the pieces, making them easier for young children to grasp. Puzzles often include simple shapes to match that don't require a lot of manipulation or hand turning to insert them into their places. Early puzzles often have pictures at the bottom of each space to help the child match the correct piece to its spot. As children develop, the puzzles appropriate for their age will no longer have handles on the pieces, and the pieces themselves will be smaller. As children advance in their skills, they will need to use the picture the puzzle's box to manipulate and interlock many pieces together to finish both tabletop and floor puzzles.

Here are some puzzles to try, in order from easiest to more challenging, based upon a child's age:

- Geometric Puzzle Board by Kaplan Early Learning
- Chunky Puzzle Set by Melissa & Doug (available on Kaplan Early Learning site)
- Peg puzzles by Melissa & Doug
- Puzzle Cards by Learning Resources
- Sea Life Floor Puzzle by Kaplan Early Learning

Blocks

Around eight months of age, babies learn to use large, soft stacking blocks, which are easier to hold and safe for mouthing and exploration while babies are working on their grasp and release patterns. Magnetic blocks can also offer a little support for children learning to release with control while stacking; the pull of the magnets will help the blocks balance and stay on top of one another. Large Mega Bloks are still safe for toddlers who like to throw and are easy to pull apart and put back together. Duplo Building Bricks by Lego begin the transition from stacking blocks to more intricate brick-building as children follow step-by-step instructions to create simple builds.

One-inch standard wooden blocks are helpful for expanding visual motor skills by making block designs. These blocks are often seen in standardized tests, in which children use them to recreate towers, trains, steps, and pyramids. Larger wooden block sets help children understand how to use their imaginations to create larger structures.

The most complicated blocks are classic Lego sets. Some children are skilled enough to create their own designs, while others benefit from picture manuals that offer step-by-step instructions to create characters and scenes. The smaller the blocks, the more intricate the needed hand muscles. Using these muscles helps promote children's hand strength and skill.

Blocks can be used to teach activities in a step-by-step way. Stack a few blocks in a tower or do a simple build, then ask the child to copy you. This is a great way to build imagination with blocks. Not all children can just make amazing structures; many need a demonstration or a picture card or manual to look at.

Here are some of the best block choices, in order from easy to more challenging:

- Baby teether blocks
- Magnetic Wooden Blocks by Tegu
- Mega Bloks by Mattel
- Duplo Building Bricks by Lego
- 1-inch blocks by Learning Resources
- Standard Unit Blocks by Kaplan Early Learning
- Classic Bricks by Lego

One-Inch Blocks

I'm a big fan of small, colorful, one-inch wooden cube blocks. They are a great size to fit in the palm of a child's hand without being too big or too small. A large container of these blocks is not too expensive, and they can be used to help teach so many other concepts. They even "grow" along with the child. At first, babies as young as one year can work on holding one block in each hand and banging them together. After achieving that skill, the blocks are the perfect size for the child to work on stacking them to create a tower.

- **Make it easier:** For a baby learning to stack blocks, hold a block near their hand so they can pick it up. If the ability to let go easily isn't there yet, teach them about stacking by placing a block on a table. Give the child a block to hold in their hand, then hold their wrist in position while they are holding the block over the one on the table. While you support their hand, encourage them to let go. If they do so, they will have the success of releasing one block on top of another to.

- **Make it harder:** For children who have mastered creating block towers and moving blocks into and out of a container, work on making simple block designs with three or four blocks. Make a design yourself, then give the child blocks that are the same colors and shapes and encourage the child to make your design. For children who want to take it one step further, see if they will copy your design using blocks of the same shapes but different colors, putting them in the same positions as the blocks in your design.

Magna-Tiles

Magna-Tiles are colored shapes that come in different sizes and have magnets on the edges. They can be used to build structures, boats, castles, towers, trains, barns, parking garages, and basically anything else a child's imagination can create. The pull of the magnets is strong and can make it challenging for children to just take them apart when building. However, using Magna-Tiles is a good activity for working on visual motor skills as children use pictures and existing designs as models for their own designs.

- **Make it easier:** Some children don't have the ability to imagine structures as easily as others do and need help to create designs. Create two sets of Magna-Tiles—one for you and one for the child you're working with—that have sixteen tiles each (eight squares and eight triangles). Demonstrate how to use the tiles to make a box with a triangular roof. Stop after adjoining each tile and give the child time to imitate you. After they've practiced, encourage them to make a box on their own.
- **Make it harder:** Create two identical sets of tiles, one for you and one for the child. Build a structure and see if the child can copy it. Or create a model for them to imitate, but give them too many pieces and shapes of different colors from the ones you used. This way, the child has to sort through the tiles and choose the best ones.

Pegboards

Pegboards are a visual motor activity that works on skilled grasp and release patterns, which begin to develop when children are about the age of one and continue developing into their elementary years. These can help build the mature tripod grasp needed for writing.

At first, use pegboards designed for younger children, which have large and chunky pieces along with openings in the boards that are round and easy to insert pegs into. More challenging pegboards have smaller pieces and insertion holes that require more force and control. Lots of children enjoy using pegboards with templates, such as button-art toys, where they can match different colored pegs to holes to create a picture. As children get older and their spatial awareness improves, they can use small pegboards to imagine and create unique pictures. These smaller, more intricate pegs really work on developing intricate grasp patterns and hand strength.

Foam Pegboards

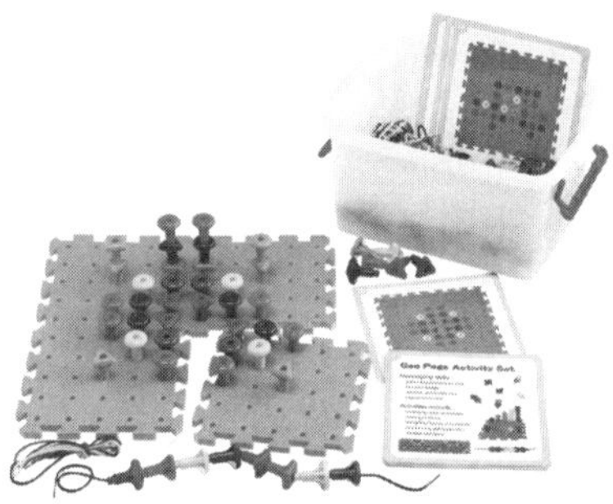

Foam pegboards are a great fine motor activity to work on grasp and release patterns. Children put the pegs into and pull them out of the foam board. Depending on the child's hand strength and skill, pegboards offer opportunities for skill growth.

- **Make it easier:** Insert the pegs into the pegboard and invite the children to remove the pegs and place them in a storage bag or container. Or don't use the formboard, and just hold one peg and ask the children stack more on top to create a tower. They can then pull the pegs apart and place them into a container.
- **Make it harder:** Use the pegs to create a sequence in the top line of the pegboard. Then, invite the children to use the second row to match the colors of your sequence. Many pegboards also come with picture cards that correspond to a diagram. These photos can help children follow a sequence as they place the pegs in the proper locations to match the image. An even more challenging skill is to create sequences that are stacked and have dimension.

Just like many of the other toys listed in this chapter, pegboards also come in different sizes and can be used with different age groups. With younger children, start with larger pieces so children must use their whole hand to grasp the peg. Advance to smaller, more intricate pieces that require a lot more skill and strength to be inserted into a pegboard.

The following are some of the best pegboards for children, starting with easy ones and moving to more challenging ones as children improve their stacking skills and unleash some imagination and creativity to design interesting pictures. Remember the classic Lite-Brite? That activity is the most advanced pegboard. The board itself is in a vertical position like an easel, which requires a child to have or develop wrist strength and the ability to hold tiny pegs while using enough force to pierce the paper to copy the design.

- My First Pegs by Quercetti
- Spike the Fine Motor Hedgehog by Learning Resources
- Pegboards by Skoolzy
- Button Art Activity Set by Alex Toys
- FantaColor Design by Quercetti
- Lite-Brite

Spike the Fine Motor Hedgehog

This is a versatile pegboard initially meant for young children. All the pegs are large and multicolored, but there is no wrong hole to insert them into because they all have rounded bottoms. Many children will sit and pick up the pieces, then need to turn the pegs around to insert them into the hole correctly.

- **Make it easier:** Hand the child the pegs, or place one in their hand, one by one in such a way that they can grasp each peg with their fingers and insert it into any opening. Giving them one piece at a time and helping them with the proper grasp pattern will help teach them about success and build their confidence to insert all the pegs.
- **Make it harder:** Spike the Hedgehog has red, purple, orange, and green pegs. Leaving the pegs in a big pile on the table or on the floor near the child will require that the child pick each piece up, orient it by turning and flipping it around, then insert it into a hole. Many children need support to pick the correct end to insert. The different colored pegs can also be used to design a simple sequence that a child can copy. For much older children, if you look closely at Spike's shell, there are different numbers. For a child who has developed number recognition, ask them to put a peg in an opening with a specific number. Make the activity even harder by encouraging them to put a specific colored peg in a specific location.

Stringing Beads

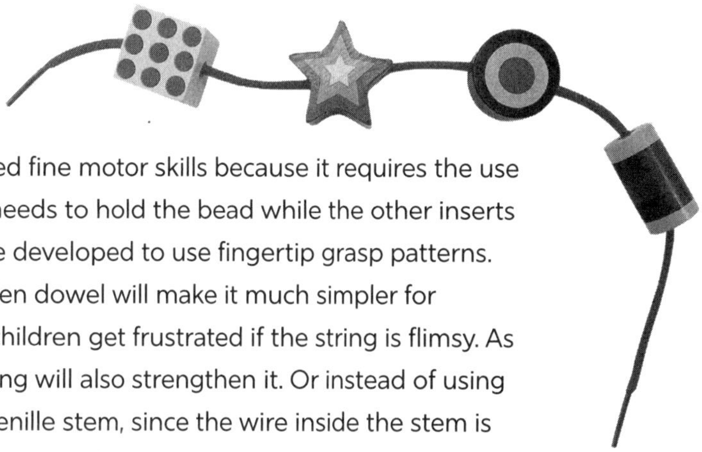

Stringing beads is one of the most advanced fine motor skills because it requires the use of two hands at the same time: one hand needs to hold the bead while the other inserts a string. For control, both hands need to be developed to use fingertip grasp patterns. Using a string with one end tied to a wooden dowel will make it much simpler for children to start stringing beads, as many children get frustrated if the string is flimsy. As a quick fix, adding tape around a flimsy string will also strengthen it. Or instead of using a string, children can slide beads onto a chenille stem, since the wire inside the stem is sturdy and the beads are more likely to remain on the stem. This is easier for younger children to manage. Using larger, square beads is easier than holding smaller, round beads. Over time, when children get the concept of inserting a string into beads, they can complete more challenging activities as they follow bead patterns on cards. Pony beads are the smallest beads and are frequently used in arts and crafts projects; pony beads challenge a child's ability to use a refined fingertip grasp.

Here are some specific toys that encourage success with bead stringing. Items in the list are in order from simple to more challenging.

- Dowel Bead Stringing Activities by Haba
- Traditional beads with loose string
- Beads and Pattern Cards Activity Set by Learning Resources
- Pony beads by Kaplan Early Learning

★ ★ ★

This chapter includes many of my favorite toys for younger children. As an OT, I am skilled at understanding the progression of toys and activities from easiest to hardest. Finding that just-right challenge can be difficult for some children, especially since many have skill levels that are inconsistent. Teachers may want to try to improve a child's grasp patterns through coloring and writing, but children who struggle with fine motor skills don't like to write or color. Because they do not have the proper grasp patterns, some children may find these activities difficult and just not fun. In the next chapter, I share with you some of my favorite tips to build fine motor skills by pairing some common household items with simple sensory play.

CHAPTER 6:

Building Advanced Visual Motor Skills without Pencil and Paper

Sensory bins are common in early childhood classrooms. Lots of children enjoy finding small toys hidden in sensory containers full of mediums such as playdough, sand, water beads, water, shredded paper, leaves, aquarium rocks, stones, birdseed, and cotton balls. They use their hands as they hunt, search, scoop, and dig for the toys. Sometimes, all this scooping and dumping with sensory play makes a mess, but that's okay.

Simple additions to a sensory bin, such as household items, utensils, and tools, can add another level of skill development. For example, what if you add measuring cups with handles? Now children are working on the added skill of scooping, which improves their grasp patterns and wrist control as they scoop and dump. What if you add a funnel? A child can use one hand to hold the funnel and the other hand to hold a measuring cup to scoop and pour into the funnel. This activity improves their bilateral coordination—using both hands at the same time—which we talked about in chapter 3.

Many children prefer to use only their dominant hand in sensory bins, while the other hand stays up in the air or on their lap. Their nondominant hand is the "helper hand." Watch how children are playing, and encourage them to use their helper hands to hold another toy or the side of the bin, so that both hands are involved. Bilateral coordination is important because it's required when completing more challenging school skills. For example, when a child is cutting with scissors, the nondominant hand must hold and rotate the paper so the child can cut accurately. If you can find interesting activities for sensory bins that also work on bilateral-coordination skills, children will improve their grasp patterns while having fun, too.

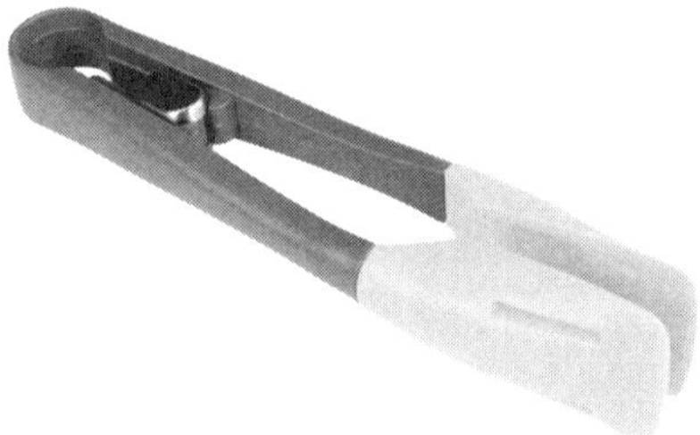

What other tools can you add to a sensory bin? Add a pair of toaster tongs, and now a child can use the tongs to work on picking up and returning cotton balls to a container for cleanup. This skill is a direct parallel to the grasp pattern children need to hold a pencil. Using tongs to build this skill is a lot more fun than just having to color or to write letters over and over again.

If you have a big bin of interlocking cubes or small blocks with letters, why not try adding them to a sensory bin? Encourage children to pick them up and sort them with scoops or tweezers. Then, they can connect the blocks or cubes to spelling their names or common sight words.

The key to helping a child improve their bilateral coordination is to understand the types of skills an individual child or class needs to work on, then advance them over time. Don't be afraid to try different activities. Some will work better than others, but finding novel activities keeps everyone motivated. I guarantee you will stumble onto something that becomes a crowd pleaser.

And these activities don't just have to be used in a sensory bin, either—use your imagination and your resources.

Tools for Specific Skills

Let's explore some tools you can use to help children with specific fine and visual motor skills. There are some unique toys and items that can be used to target the development of specific skills. I've listed some of my favorites under the applicable skills.

Bilateral Coordination

Often found in discount stores, the following common household tools will help children begin to use two hands at the same time when scooping and interacting with items:

- Salad tongs
- Rolling pins
- Large liquid syringes

Using Scissors

Add some of these tools to the sensory bin to aid children's scissor use. The tools listed mimic using the proper scissor grasp with the control to open and close—without the sharp edges of a pair of scissors.

- Bunny-shaped egg dippers
- Meat-baller scoops
- Colorful Handy Scoops by Kaplan Early Learning

Developing Hand-Muscle Strength

The following tools help build intrinsic muscle strength in children's hands. Encourage children to use these tools like a marker or pencil: by holding the tool with a dynamic tripod grasp pattern, with their thumb and index and middle fingers while flexing the ring and pinky fingers into the palm.

- Toaster tongs
- Silicone Mini Tongs by Kaplan Early Learning
- All-Weather Jumbo Tweezers by Kaplan Early Learning
- Strawberry hullers
- Super Sorting Pie by Learning Resources

To build basic hand strength, add tools for sensory play that have one rounded end for scooping and dumping and one end to squeeze.

- Squeezy Tweezers by Kaplan Early Learning
- Tea-bag infusers

Super Sorting Pie

Per the product directions, children are encouraged to use the tweezers to sort the various colorful fruits into the pie sorter by color, shape, or amount.

- **Make it easier:** Take away the tweezers and encourage the children to just use their fingers. You can also start with basic color-matching options before having children discriminate by shape or count out a specific number of fruits.
- **Make it harder:**
    - Swap out the tweezers for a tea-bag infuser that requires more strength to squeeze.
    - If children need to develop better scissor skills, try giving them a kitchen meat-baller tool or bunny tongs. These require the children to open and close the handles to pick up the items when sorting them.
    - Work on children's palm-to-finger translation and in-hand manipulation by handing the children two different-colored items to hold in the tweezers at the same time. Ask them to release each item into its correct space while trying not to drop the other item.

Looking for something fun for the water table? Tools with a bulb-type end to squeeze are a great addition.

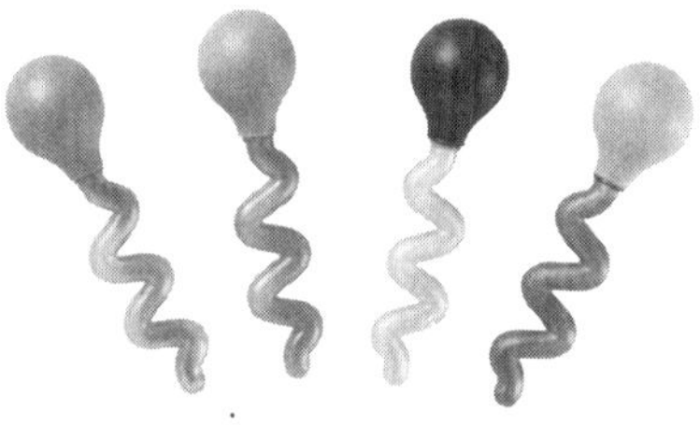

- Twisty Droppers by Kaplan Early Learning
- Turkey basters
- Eyedroppers

Storage Bins and Containers for Tools

The tools and manipulatives described in this chapter (and other small toys) can be difficult to manage and clean up, as they get easily thrown or dumped out of open containers. While ziplock bags can do the job, you can create a storage system for supplies that also has a built-in fine motor component. Here are some ideas I've used in the classroom and at home.

- **Twist-and-lock and snap-lock containers:** Tired of opening and closing everyone's containers at lunch or snack? Using containers like these for tools and manipulatives will also help build children's confidence as they work on the same activities in their play. They can then generalize these skills to their self-help skills later on.
- **Slider bags:** These are easy to find in any store, but choose the ones with plastic sliders across the top for more skill building. Many children struggle with closing traditional resealable plastic bags.

- **Reuseable zipper pouches:** These come in all sizes. Large pouches are a great storage option for puzzles so the pieces remain with their puzzles and don't get lost.
- **Small plastic storage bins with lids**
- **Clear plastic jars with built-in handles:** These are perfect for activities with lots of pieces.
- **Recycled grated-cheese containers:** These are a fantastic storage option. I use these for small fidget toys and small crayons because the end with three holes is fun for children to put crayons into and out of. The pieces can easily be removed by just pulling off the lid or trying to shake them out. The lids are also a good workout for hands to pull up and push down.
- **Spice containers:** These small containers are perfect for glitter and other arts-and-crafts supplies. Spice containers work well because the lids need to be twisted using wrist rotation, which is more difficult than lifting one edge of a lid and removing it by pulling.
- **Containers with pull-off lids:** These are classic storage items similar to the types of containers used for packing lunches and snacks brought from home.
- **Take-out deli containers:** I make toys out of these to leave around for children so they can work on specific skills. Using a pair of scissors, cut small circular openings in the container, or cut an X shape that is fun to push blocks and beads into. Make sure there are no sharp edges before you let children play with the cut containers.

★ ★ ★

Some children have an aversion to any pencil-and-paper tasks that seem like work, and this can lead to some tricky behaviors to manage. Rest assured that incorporating these fun tools into activities actually helps to build the same underlying skills that writing does, but children will find these activities more exciting and will easily engage with them when using sensory mediums or bins. Bonus: Some of these tools and containers can be used in games to enhance the play or with arts-and-crafts activities.

CHAPTER 7:

Visual Motor Skills for Self-Care

While visual motor skills for handwriting and academic skills often gain a lot of attention, self-care skills are also important. Self-care skills are needed for day-to-day tasks that involve using fine motor grasping and eye-hand coordination, such as the following:

- Handwashing
- Manipulating containers to squeeze out or pump soap
- Putting on and taking off clothes
- Managing fasteners such as Velcro, zippers, buttons, and snaps
- Tying shoelaces
- Scooping and spearing food with utensils such as spoons and forks
- Spreading and cutting food with a knife
- Drinking from an open cup
- Using two hands to cut food with a fork and knife
- Opening snack packages, containers, and resealable bags
- Putting toothpaste on a toothbrush and brushing teeth
- Managing clothing and wiping when toileting

Let's look at some of the most common self-help tasks—including handwashing, getting dressed, eating and drinking, and toothbrushing—and how you can support children in developing the visual motor skills needed to accomplish these tasks.

Handwashing

Handwashing is one of the first self-care activities children engage in, starting at very early ages.

At one to two years of age, children will reach their arms out under a stream of water and begin to bring their hands together and rub them to clean them. Between the ages of three and a half to four, most children can complete all steps of handwashing thoroughly. Singing songs and providing visuals and demonstrations will help children learn these skills more easily and perform them with more thoroughness. You can also teach children to wipe their hands with a baby wipe as an alternative when soap and water aren't available. Managing full-sized containers to squeeze or pump out soap to wash hands, faces, and bodies or to shampoo hair can be hard for little hands. Using trial-sized containers that are smaller and require less force enables children to have more success and accuracy when squeezing or pumping out soap.

Getting Dressed

Learning how to dress oneself is among the hardest visual motor skills to teach. Some children just don't like using and manipulating fasteners. When these are on clothes the child is wearing, the task is not easy, especially if children don't quite have the strength or the attention to persist until they succeed.

To encourage reluctant children to engage in the task of getting dressed, consider adding materials to the classroom, such as fine motor activity books, quiet books, Montessori busy boards, and buckle pillows. These often have fun dressing activities that offer playful ways to practice using buttons, zippers, snaps, and buckles. Dressing boards are another strategy to help children practice using zippers, buttons, snaps, or Velcro while sitting at a table. After children have practiced using a dressing board, introduce dressing vests. Place these in dress-up corners so children can have fun experimenting with all the different fasteners.

With many of these tasks, it's important to break down each into smaller components, sometimes offering some accommodations and tips that make complicated skills easier. Doing so will help improve children's participation and build confidence. The following are some ways to help children learn to use Velcro, zippers, buttons, snaps, and shoelaces.

Hook-and-Loop Closures

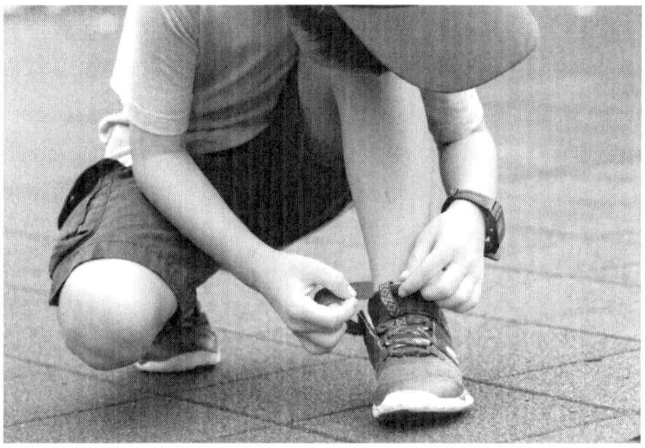

Independently putting on and taking off shoes with hook-and-loop closures, such as Velcro, occurs around four and a half to five years of age. But most children can pull simple pieces of Velcro on and off of toys and other items around the age of two. One of the first self-care skills children encounter that requires fine motor skills is managing the Velcro on their shoes. Once the Velcro pieces are aligned, pushing the top strap down to attach it is easier than using strength to pull it up. Some children get frustrated if the strap reattaches when they are trying to pull it up to take their shoes off. If you help them, place your finger on the soft part of the Velcro from which the top strap has already been removed, as this will block it from unexpectedly reattaching and can minimize children's frustration.

Zippers

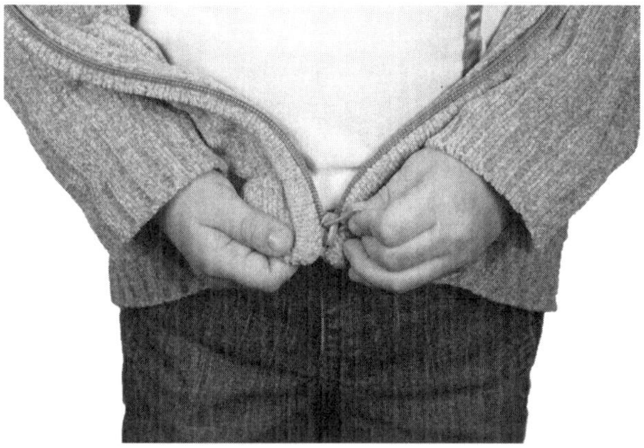

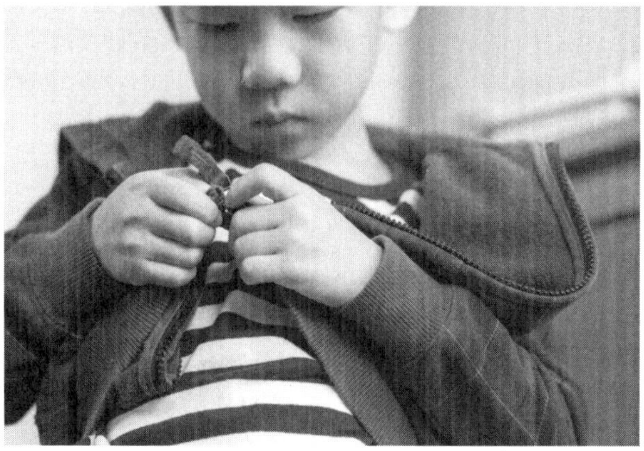

When it comes to zippers, before you jump right into teaching children how to zip up a jacket, start with having them open and close small makeup bags, backpacks, lunch boxes, and three-quarter-zip sweatshirts on which the zipper does not need to be attached first. It's also easier for children to pull a zipper down vertically than to pull it horizontally or from the bottom to the top. For a child who has a hard time just grasping the small zipper pull on clothing or using a pull once they do grasp it, add a ring or a keychain so they can find the slider and pull it up and down the track. At age two and a half, a child can pull a zipper down to take off their coat. However, aligning and connecting a zipper at the bottom can take some time and practice. At the ages of five and a half to six, a child is generally able to align and hook the pieces of a zipper, grasp the pull, and move the slider up and down all by themselves.

Putting a coat or a dressing board on a table is a great way to let children practice aligning and hooking the pieces of a zipper, then pulling it up the track. Using consistent verbal cues such as "Put the train all the way in the station" can help remind children of the steps they need to take.

If you are purchasing outerwear for young children, resist the urge to buy jackets that are too big or bulky—extra fabric is hard for little children to manage and causes a lot of frustration (for them and for adults).

Case Study: Helping Children Zip Up Their Coats

It's a cold day at school but still warm enough to head outside for playtime. As the children are getting ready, you notice that DaShawn and Lily are struggling with putting on their coats, and everyone else is getting impatient, frustrated, and hot. How can you teach children how to manage fasteners such as zippers?

Aligning and connecting zippers is not easy. A simple way to start practicing is to align and connect the zipper for a child and then encourage them to pull the zipper from the bottom of the jacket to the top. Attaching a keychain or ring to the zipper pull is an easy way to help children to grasp it.

You can also have children practice zippering their jackets ahead of time, before everyone is lining up to go outside. Ask the children to sit down and put their jackets in front of them on a table. Position each child's jacket so the top is nearest to the child. Tell the children that a zipper is like a train—it needs to connect to its track. Show them how to place the bottom of the slider completely against the bottom stop so the slider will smoothly travel up the track. At first, you might need to support a child by holding one of their hands firmly at the bottom of the zipper while their other hand pulls the zipper up. Keeping one hand steady at the bottom while the other pulls up requires bilateral coordination. It's not an easy concept for many children to gain. For a child who is struggling, have them sit down to practice while wearing their coat; this way, they can shift their gaze down and focus on proper alignment of the zipper parts. Managing zippers will take a lot of visual attention and practice before children can connect the pieces and quickly zip without looking

Buttons

Buttoning is a complicated skill that requires children to use both of their hands at the same time: one hand to insert the button correctly into the hole on the opposite side, and the other hand to pinch and pull the button all the way through using strength.

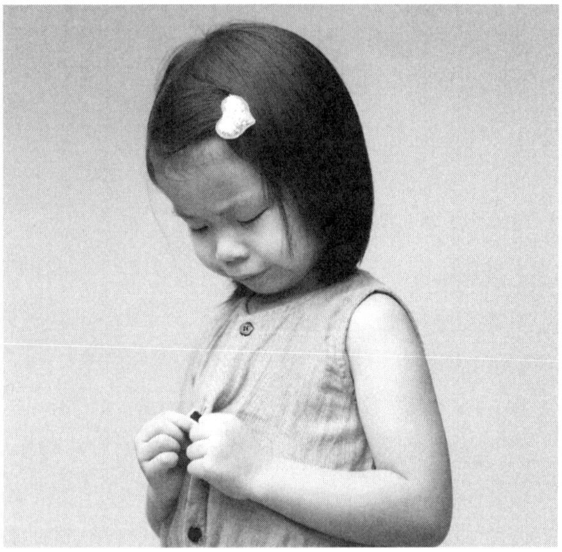

Larger buttons are easier to hold and manage in comparison to the smaller buttons that are generally on button-down shirts. At two and a half years of age, many children can button a large button, but it takes them until they are about four or four and a half to have the hand strength and skill to button and unbutton most button sizes. Using button strips, button boards, or even old clothing laid on a table helps children practice buttoning before they try it while wearing clothing that has buttons.

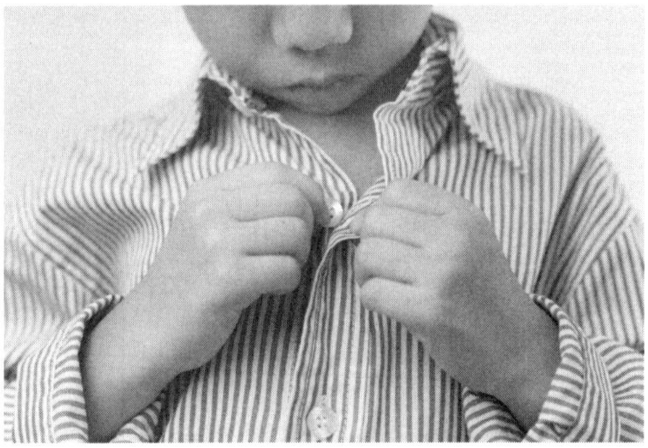

Sometimes, starting with the bottom button on a shirt is easier than starting from the top, because children can see the bottom buttons easily. Sitting in a chair to complete buttoning is also easier than manipulating buttons while standing, at least for those who have core muscle weakness. Using a plastic take-out container with a vertical slit cut into the top is another way for children to practice manipulating a button into a vertical position and using their strength to push the button through.

Snaps

Most children can align and manipulate snaps by the ages of three and a half or four years old. Lots of children try to use an index finger to push a snap against their chest to secure it. Aligning snaps requires a three-jaw chuck grasp pattern (discussed in chapter 4) on both hands to grab the pieces of the snaps, position them, and squish them together to fasten them. Using a three-jaw chuck pattern to place both thumbs on the top of the snap and the fingers behind it will make snapping easier than using only one hand.

Build hand and pinch strength specifically for snaps by encouraging children to squish resistive TheraPutty with their fingertips in a three-jaw chuck pattern. They can also squeeze clothespins to build strength and coordination needed for snapping. Snap-block animals or vehicles, available from Guidecraft and Kaplan Early Learning, are a good way to encourage hand and pinch strength.

Buckles

Buckles commonly found on booster chairs, high chairs, and seatbelts can fasten easily but require a significant amount of pressure, usually with both hands, to release. Buckles are critical for safely securing children to prevent them from falling or being injured in an accident. Consider a child's maturity level before teaching them how to unbuckle. For older children with weaker hand strength, or even for adults who struggle with unbuckling, special tools are available that make unbuckling easier. These tools are often used by families to let their older children unbuckle themselves quickly, especially in car lines, speeding up the process of getting out of the car.

Shoe Tying

Children who are in kindergarten (ages five and up) can usually tie their shoes, provided they are not delayed in their fine motor skills. Shoe tying is a complicated skill. Not only does it require complicated actions that need to be completed in a sequence, but also there are so many steps that children who have attention concerns need extra instruction and practice to learn the process. Using specific verbal cues when teaching shoe tying can be helpful for sequencing. Some children with developmental delays don't fully understand this concept until they are older; they will likely master this task closer to the ages of seven or eight.

Here are some ideas on how to help children learn to tie their shoes:

- First, try teaching shoe tying with the traditional method. The child creates one loop with the shoelace, pinches it at the bottom, uses their opposite hand to run the free end of the lace around the base of the loop, pushes the end under the part that is now wrapped around the loop, and then pinches and pulls both loops for a bow. The age-old "bunny ears" method can be more difficult than others because both hands need to perform some actions at the same time.

- If the traditional method is not successful, YouTube offers step-by-step videos that can help children practice each small step.
- Have a child sit in a chair (rather than on the floor) with one foot on a footrest, which helps them see their shoe more clearly and stabilizes their body.
- Encourage a child to practice with a shoe in front of them (instead of on their foot), either on their lap or on a table. Turn the shoe so the heel is positioned closest to the child, in the same orientation as if they were wearing it.
- Offer two different-colored laces to help children see the differences in how the laces move.
- Use backward chaining. You, the adult, complete all the steps except the last one. The child finishes the task and has the success of completion. Then, try again but stop before completing the last two steps. Allow the child to complete those. Continue until the child can successfully complete all the steps.

If a child is really struggling, use Velcro or slip-on shoes, or modify the existing shoes to include elastic-type laces that do not need to be tied. Also known as "lock laces," these can accommodate children who are not able to successfully tie their shoes.

Eating and Drinking

Babies learn to finger-feed themselves with a raking grasp; they pick up the food using the pinky side of their hand, bring the food to their mouth, then push it in with the palm. The next step is a neat pincer grasp, using the thumb and index finger. To promote a neat pincer grasp, offer a child just a few pieces of dry cereal or goldfish crackers

at a time on their tray. The bigger the pile, the higher the chance the child will want to pick them all up and shove them in their mouth. Another trick is to hand the child pieces one by one. Hold each piece up in the air in front of them. The child will reach out to take the piece, which slows them down, and they often use a more accurate grasp pattern than when they try to pick up an item off the tray.

Around one year of age, children learn to scoop a spoon into purees or yogurt and begin to feed themselves. In this phase, hand-over-hand support—in which an adult holds their hand over the child's hand to guide it, dips the spoon into the bowl, and brings the food to the child's mouth while the child removes the food with their lips—will help with motor planning so the child can feel how to use their muscles in that pattern and recreate it.

Case Study: Helping Jordyn Use the Pincer Grasp to Feed Herself

At snack, Jordyn is picking up her goldfish crackers and shoving several into her mouth with her palm before chewing. How can you get Jordyn to use a neat pincer grasp?

Offer her just a few crackers at a time, and model for her how to pinch her thumb and index finger together to get them. Hold one cracker in the air and encourage her to reach for it with either hand. See if she orients her hand with her thumb and index finger and uses a more refined grasp pattern with this strategy.

Alternatively, try putting Jordyn's goldfish crackers in a line on a paper towel, then encouraging her to eat them one at a time, starting on the left and moving across the row to the right.

Spoons

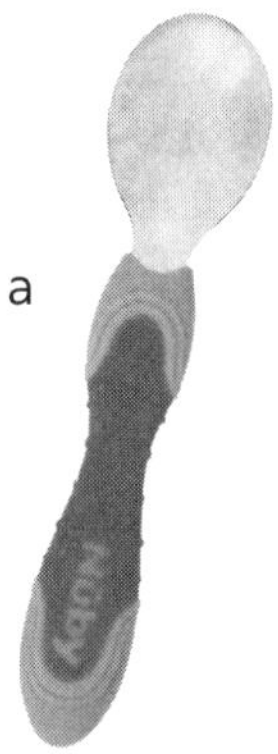

Using a spoon to explore self-feeding begins at the age of ten or eleven months. By age two and a half, children are generally able to scoop food with a spoon and feed themselves with minimal spilling. By the age of four, they are generally using their fingertips to support the spoon for more control, rather than using a palmar grasp that offers less control. Spoons with shorter, fatter, curved handles and metal bowls are easier to manage than full-size metal or plastic utensils.

Starting with thicker foods, such as yogurt, is easier because they stick to the spoon. Placing a spoon into a taller container, such as a yogurt container, will encourage some children to grasp the spoon, take it out of the container, and bring it to their mouth, which eliminates the need for a lot of scooping. You might also try dipping the spoon in the yogurt and handing it to a child so they can bring the spoon to their mouth to lick it off. Loading the spoon with food is the hardest part, so build children's confidence by letting them find success in getting the spoon to their mouth first. For children with weaker hand strength who lack an active grasp pattern, attach silicone grasping aids to spoons and other utensils to make it easier for children to hold them for longer periods of time without dropping them.

Forks

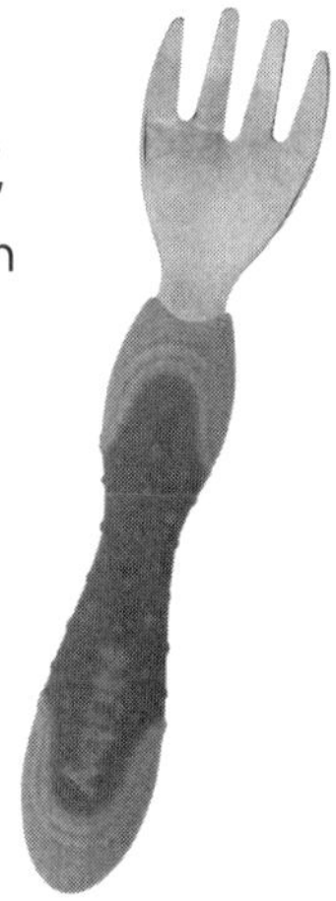

Generally, children use a spoon first, followed by a fork. By age two and a half, children are piercing foods with a fork and bringing them to their mouths with an immature palmar grasp pattern. At the age of four, children use more of a fingertip grasp pattern to pick up foods with a fork and feed themselves without spilling.

Piercing foods with a fork can be a challenge, depending on the texture of the food. Softer foods, such as canned fruits or cut-up, ripe bananas, are good choices to start with. If a child picks up a fork, guide them toward the food to pierce it, and offer a little bit of tactile support to the child's wrist. Using a fork requires a little extra strength just before the utensil pierces the food, and this small amount of stability can really make a difference.

Case Study: Helping Lily Use a Fork to Feed Herself

During lunchtime, the children are served pasta with sauce. Lily picks up a plastic disposable fork, holds it in a palmar grasp, and attempts to put the food on it by stabbing at the pasta, then awkwardly bringing it to her mouth. How do you promote a better grasp pattern for using a fork to self-feed with more control?

Holding a fork requires a fingertip grasp pattern. Activities that include using tweezers and tongs to pick up and place small objects will help promote a more advanced grasp pattern. Instruct Lily on holding the fork "in the duck's mouth." Have her imitate flexing her ring and pinky fingers into the palm of her hand while she uses a three-jaw chuck position with her thumb and index and middle fingers. After she imitates this hand posture, reposition the fork so that the part of the fork just

above the prongs is held with her fingertips. Encourage Lily to eat a few bites with this grasp pattern.

You might consider using a fork with a shorter, fatter, curved handle with metal prongs. This can also provide more success in piercing the food; plastic utensils can be awkward and flimsy.

If it's hard for Lily to pierce the food on her own, offer hand-over-hand support to help her load the food onto the fork, then let her bring the fork the rest of the way to her mouth to use her lips to remove the food from the utensil. You can also load the fork with food yourself and place it on the edge of her plate. Encourage her to pick up the fork with her fingers by coming underneath it while it hangs off the plate, then to self-feed that way for some success.

Knives

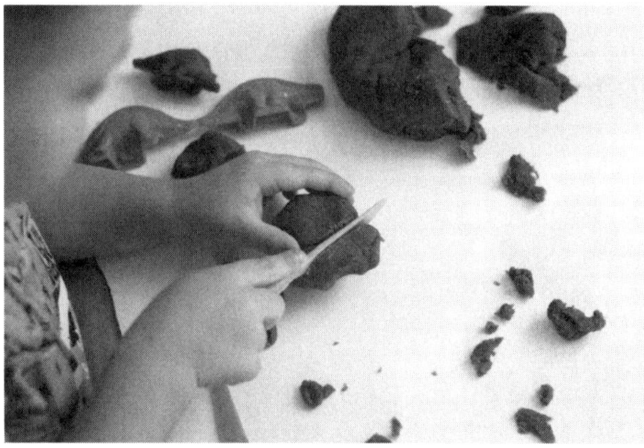

One of the first steps to using a knife is cutting or chopping during play. "Cutting" Velcro fruit and veggies or using a small plastic knife with playdough are common activities to begin exposure.

Spreading with a knife occurs around five years of age. Cutting softer foods happens at five and a half, while using enough force to safely cut through foods, such as meat, occurs between seven and eight years. By about the age of eight, children should be able to use a fork and a knife at the same time to cut foods.

Learning knife skills requires a lot of support and safety. Model how to hold a knife, and keep your hand steady while sawing back and forth to cut through the food or sensory items. Teaching knife safety is also important, and using toys and safer activities first is always a good idea to make sure children are mature enough to engage in learning. Some butter knives are long and heavy and difficult to spread with; a dull, decorative spreader with a rounded end can be much easier for children to control.

Using a fork and a knife at the same time is the most difficult skill, as the fork needs to be inserted into the food and stabilized with one hand while the other uses sawing motions to cut. Video modeling—watching others use a fork and knife to cut in a video—can help some children preview the activity and perform it safely with improved coordination.

Again, child-sized forks and knives with metal ends are generally the best choices when teaching children to cut more challenging foods.

Open-Cup Drinking

Holding a heavy cup full of water or juice and drinking from it can lead to lots of spills. Around age three and a half, most children can use one hand to pick up a cup and take a drink without spilling it. This is why younger children use sippy cups and straw cups.

Worried about making too much of a mess? Try using small paper cups (the bathroom size) or even a plastic medicine cup with just a little bit of fluid or a thicker puree. The thicker puree won't move as quickly as a pure liquid, making it easier to manage. Young children can generally hold these cups with one hand and control them more easily to tip them up while drinking. Until children are proficient, 360-degree sippy cups are also a good option, as they simulate open-cup drinking without the mess.

Opening Snack Packages, Containers, and Resealable Bags

Packages of chips, cheese sticks, and other snacks can be a real challenge for children with weaker fine motor skills to open. Instead of getting in the habit of opening packages for them, demonstrate how to pinch and pull the top open just a little, then encourage the children to finish the job themselves. Resealable bags can be hard to pull apart. Again, starting it just a little or using slide-top bags is generally easier. For children who can safely use scissors, as a last resort you can show them how to use a pair of scissors to snip off one of the corners of a package.

Toothbrushing

At four and a half years of age, most children can remove or open the toothpaste cap, apply toothpaste to a toothbrush, and brush their teeth thoroughly. Some toothpaste containers use a twist-off cap; others require the child to use enough force to pop the top back or to push down on a pump. Finding a tube with a cap that matches the child's skills and abilities is helpful for independence.

Unlocking a cap so children can just flip it open, or twisting a cap three-fourths of the way off prior to giving the toothpaste to a child will help build confidence. Resting a toothbrush on the counter is also easier than trying to squeeze the tube in one hand and hold the toothbrush in the other because some children might need two hands at the same time to squeeze the toothpaste out. For children with weaker hand strength, there are even wall-mounted automatic toothpaste dispensers, too.

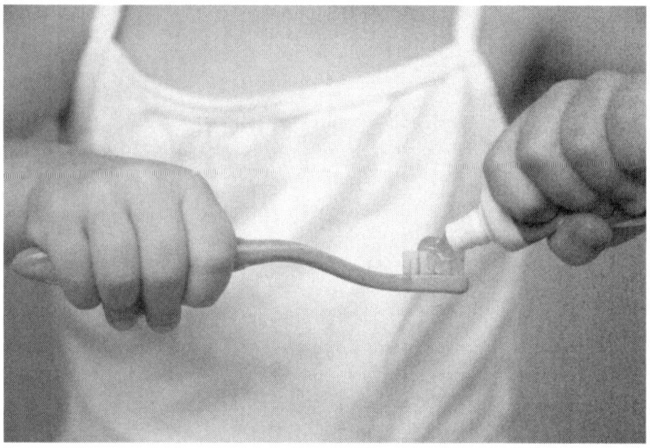

If children lack strength in their arms and upper bodies, it can be difficult for them to manage back-and-forth motions to brush each quadrant of the mouth thoroughly. Using vibrating or electric toothbrushes is a great way to help children who lack strength and control to be more thorough and effective.

★ ★ ★

In the previous chapters, we have looked in depth at how important visual motor skills are for a child every day when playing and completing their self-help skills. In the next chapter, we learn how to support preschool children in a very important visual motor skill that they will take to school and beyond—using scissors.

CHAPTER 8:
Building Scissor Cutting Skills

We have explored the crucial role of visual motor skills in play and self-care tasks. As children advance in honing these skills, they also gain the ability to apply them to school-readiness tasks, such as using scissors. When children cut with scissors, they strengthen their hand muscles as well as develop their bilateral coordination skills and visual motor and fine motor skills.

Types of Scissors

When children are younger, scissors that are meant for them will work no matter whether a child uses their right hand or left hand. However, as children advance in their scissor skills, they will need scissors that are appropriate for their age and skill level. The following is a progression of scissors, starting with ones suitable for toddlers and moving into elementary school ages. It is important to match the right pair of scissors with the skill level of the child.

Toddler Spring-Loaded Scissors

For toddlers, I recommend spring-loaded scissors, such as those made by Harac (available on Amazon.com). These scissors will work whether a child wants to use their right hand or their left hand. They are sharp and capable of cutting skin, so consider keeping the plastic guards on the ends of the blades, and position the paper inside the opening for children who are excitable or impulsive. These scissors make a satisfying snipping sound when cutting. Lots of people, including children and adults, really enjoy using these scissors. The spring pops up and makes it easier for children to master the underlying motor pattern of opening and closing their hands. It's also easy to use these scissors in a hand-over-hand fashion for children who are learning to cut with accuracy. When using hinged or loop scissors, the teacher can hold their hand over the child's and squeeze. This way, the child can feel what their hands should be doing. The teacher's other hand can also hold the child's "helper hand" to support the paper.

Cueing

Cueing can help a child engage in an activity they might just be learning about and do not have strong skills in, as it offers strategies combined with motivation to help them participate. There are different types of cueing: verbal and physical (or tactile).

Verbal cueing is when you offer words of encouragement such as, "Watch me!" "Do this!" or "Keep going! Great job!" I often use verbal cueing with short phrases, such as singing, "Open, shut them. Open, shut them," while squeezing scissors to offer a reminder of what to do. Or I create silly sayings to help a child remember a step such as, "Run the squirrel around the tree," when wrapping the lace around the loop when teaching shoe tying. Tip: Don't use a lot of words. Children can get overwhelmed with verbal cueing, so keep the instructions short, direct, and clear.

Physical cueing, also called *tactile cueing*, relates to using your hands to show children what to do or how you expect them to engage in an activity. Hand-over-hand support is a type of physical cueing. Sometimes, I perform the action as a demonstration, then give a child the blocks or items and wait for them to imitate what I just did. If the child picks up a block to try but isn't sure of the next step, I might touch, tap, or point to the top of another block to show them where to place the first one. When I teach children how to string beads, I might give them a string in one hand and a bead in the other. Using hand-over-hand support, I might take the hand with the string and insert it into the bead, then tap the hand holding the bead and point to the string to cue the child to let go and grab the end of the string to pull it through. I might pair the physical cue with a verbal cue and say, "Push," while inserting it and "Pull" when it emerges. As children gain more skill, you can vary your prompts to further build children's skills and confidence. If they are doing an activity they have practiced a lot and are building the motor skills for, I might just hand them the beads, say, "Remember, push, then pull," and watch. Little cues like this can really help children confidently participate in activities that might be hard for them the first few times they try. Give them a few minutes to try a task on their own before jumping in to assist.

Mini Loop Scissors

Mini loop scissors easily fit in small hands and can be used with either the left or the right hand. Because these scissors don't have dedicated loops to separate the fingers from the thumb, it's one less thing children have to remember when they pick up the scissors. They also open and close easily but require a little more control with the paper. If the child attempts to pronate their hand—turn their thumb down toward the paper in an awkward grasp—typical scissors are more challenging to use. Mini loop scissors help to reinforce a thumbs-up hand position, which is easier to cut with. While loop scissors also come in a large size, the bigger ones are difficult for young children with small hands to hold, so make sure you are using the smaller variety.

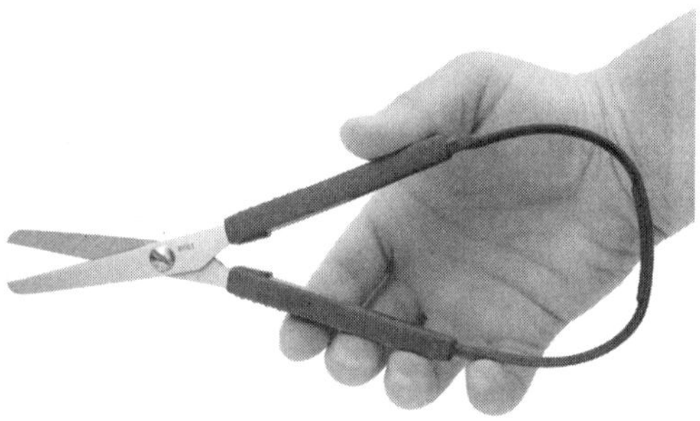

Hinged Scissors

As children begin to transition from spring-loaded or mini loop scissors, good-quality hinged scissors, such as Fiskars Training Scissors for Kids 3+ with Easy Grip, work well. As a child is learning to control the scissors, the hinge pops back open after the child squeezes their hand, so less control of finger extension is needed. As the child becomes more adept, the hinge can be flipped so the child will have to coordinate opening and closing their hands with each snip on their own. These scissors are perfect for the preschool age group because of their versatility. They have blunt tips and are generally able to cut only paper, which makes them safer for younger children or for those who can be a little more impulsive and quick with their hands. The hinge is a fun accessory to make using these scissors easier or more difficult, depending upon the child's skill level. Many blunt-tipped preschool scissors are still sharp and capable of cutting clothes and thicker papers, but rounded ends make these tools a safer choice than ones with pointed tips.

Pointed-Tip Scissors

Pointed-tip scissors are available for right-handed or left-handed users. The pointed tips allow for more accurate cutting on a line, but these scissors are the most dangerous and do require close supervision because they can cut clothes, skin, hair, and so on. Reserve these scissors for children who are in the elementary school age range or who are younger but a little more mature and becoming skilled in their scissor cutting.

Scissor Safety Tips

Incorporating scissors can be difficult when engaging children in a large group. Giving a child a pair of scissors that is too advanced for them presents the potential to do some harm if they cut themselves or their clothing. Many children can be impulsive and will quickly move or wave their hands while holding scissors near another person. Here are a few tips to keep children safe:

- Give a child a pair of safety scissors first, until you've established their scissor cutting skills and level of impulsiveness. Today's safety scissors are good enough for simple projects using regular printer or copy paper. Model scissor safety for children. Teach them how to close the scissors and grasp them with the closed blades pointing toward the floor.
- Keep a container of scissors on each table at the start of a task, rather than setting the scissors somewhere else in the classroom so that children will have to walk around with the scissors.
- Set ground rules. Even if you are offering safety scissors, treat them carefully so that, as children age and advance into higher-level skills, they take these rules with them.
- Remind children frequently that scissors are for cutting paper only, not hair or clothes. Most of the accidents I've heard about are when children get hold of scissors and use them unsupervised. Consider keeping scissors stored in containers in locked cabinets, depending on the ages and developmental levels of the children.
- If you are concerned that using scissors in a large group is hard to manage, incorporate them into a smaller center that is supervised by an adult.

Finding ways to make scissor cutting safe will make this activity successful. As children improve these skills, it also opens the door to incorporating so many fun activities into their day.

Learning How to Cut with Scissors

Now that we've considered the kinds of scissors commonly seen in an early childhood environment, we move on to the visual motor aspect of cutting with scissors. How do we get children to learn to hold their scissors in an effective way and to cut accurately with them, so they can enjoy using their scissors? The following are some of my favorite tips to help children learn to love scissor cutting.

The first step to improve visual motor skills with scissor cutting is to have children use tools such as salad tongs, meat-baller scoops, and bunny tongs. The required movements are similar to scissor cutting, but these tools are much safer for beginners and will easily engage children who might be hesitant to try scissors. You can still have dedicated time to use scissors, but make sure to add these additional tools to your sensory bins and to other activities throughout the day so children have more opportunities for practice.

Another fun activity is to rip paper. It's important to teach the skill of using two hands to rip paper, so children understand the concept of cutting even without using scissors yet. You can draw small lines on strips of paper and then encourage children to find the line and use two hands to try to rip the paper near the line. Ripping colored tissue paper, then squeezing it into little pieces and gluing them onto paper is something children enjoy, too.

The following is the typical progression of scissor skills to help you know what to expect at different levels. I'm including some ages here as a reference, but if a child you are working with has skills at a different level, find out where they are in the progression of skills, meet them where they are at, and move forward even their skill level doesn't correlate to their age. Once a child masters a step, giving them some time to complete that step confidently will help them move on to the next challenge.

How Toddlers Learn to Cut

At the age of two, toddlers can learn to snip or cut paper. They will often place one hand on each scissor loop and attempt to snip the paper while you hold it. You'll see them make one snip, then find another piece of the paper to make another snip. One snip equals opening and closing the scissors to make one cut. Toddlers frequently need help positioning their fingers accurately on top of loop scissors or inside the grips if they are using traditional preschool scissors.

For those who have mastered making snips, encourage holding the scissors in one hand and, with the thumb up and the elbow positioned against their body, they can snip around the edges of the paper to make fringe. They can also practice opening and closing their hands to cut across the paper, making multiple snips in a row, without any need for direction. It is common for young children to rotate their hand so their thumb is in a downward position in a pronated grasp pattern. This position makes it challenging to cut with accuracy. The correct grasp pattern on scissors, whether there are finger openings or not, is to put the forearm in a neutral position in which the thumb is on top.

The proper position for holding loop scissors is to put the thumb in the smaller loop, the index finger under the scissors, and the middle and ring fingers in the larger loop. This allows for more stability, control, and accuracy when cutting. For children who are unable to keep their thumbs up, encouraging them to keep their elbows, or "chicken wings," firmly against their sides or keeping their elbows "stable on the table" will help with accuracy.

Another great tip to teach children how to snip is to offer one-inch-wide, six-inch-long strips of paper. Encourage the child to hold the paper in one hand and use the hand supporting the scissors to cut the paper into multiple pieces, like confetti.

Keep those supermarket flyers that come in the mail, or rip out magazine pictures and encourage the children to sit and snip them into scraps. With no expectations from you to cut items out perfectly, this activity exposes children to the task and lets them explore it in a way that is motivating and fun.

For children who prefer even more structure or are ready to work toward cutting across a line, add some lines to the strips of paper. Spacing the lines along the length of the strip will give children a reference for where to cut and a goal to work toward. The paper should be thin enough that if they align it inside their scissors, with one squeeze they can cut through the strip easily and feel successful as they watch the paper fall to the table.

The next natural step is to offer wider paper strips, such as two inches wide instead of one inch. This will mean that the child must make two snips, one after the other, to cut across the paper. This will build the child's ability to make multiple snips in a row and eventually to cut along a line.

Preschool, Where Cutting Is Fun

At the ages of three to four, scissor cutting gets more challenging. Start children out with simple activities and provide more difficult activities over time as their skills improve. Children might not tell you they think an activity is too hard, but you'll probably realize that it is when they flat-out refuse to do it or pick up the scissors and just randomly cut across all the pictures, ignoring the lines.

Add thick, vertical lines to paper to encourage the children to work on cutting along a line, using short lines at first and progressing toward longer ones. Don't be tempted to buy lots of downloadable worksheets. You can simply draw a line with a colored marker across the paper and hand it to the child. I like to place a sticker of a child's favorite character at the top of a page and draw a straight line down from it to the bottom of the paper. I encourage the child to cut along the line to the sticker, stopping right at the bottom of it. Start with a piece of paper that is a few inches wide and has only one sticker and one line, then progress to using a standard sheet of paper with up to four stickers and four lines. Progress from straight lines to zigzag and curved lines.

Once children have mastered cutting lines, encourage them to tackle cutting shapes such as circles, squares, and triangles. Start with larger shapes and move to smaller, more intricate ones. Cutting and turning the paper is a difficult skill for many children and will require patience and practice. Precutting around shapes and giving children smaller pieces of paper to cut will also make the task easier. A general guideline is to cut within one-quarter inch of the line and move toward cutting within one-eighth inch of the line. No need to measure this with a ruler; it's just to give a reference point to see progress.

Supporting Children's Scissor Cutting Skills

Physical demonstrations in which you show children exactly what you want them to do, combined with verbal cues, will help children remember how to cut with scissors. Don't just do the following steps once. Commit to giving these reminders on how to hold the scissors and how to cut with them as many times as you need to, until all the children understand. This skill takes a lot of practice and repetition. Here are some tips on how you can help children learn this challenging skill:

- When you pick up a pair of scissors, remind children of the proper grip, and model how to hold the scissors correctly. The thumb should be in the small circular hole, the index finger in the bottom opening, and the middle finger under the hinge of the scissors. Keeping the middle finger in this position allows for more stable control of the scissors. When cutting, the elbow should ideally be against the side of the body rather than up in the air. This helps keep the hand in a thumbs-up position, which is best for cutting with control and accuracy.
- Remember that cutting and turning paper around corners and curves takes time to learn. Model for the children how to keep the scissors straight and cut to a certain point before using the opposite hand to turn the paper. Cutting from the bottom toward the top is easier than flexing, or bending, the wrist in and trying to cut from right to left across the body, which many children will definitely try at first.
- Use verbal prompts and catchy phrases, such as the following:
  - "Stable on the table" reminds children to position their elbows on the table or their forearms on the table's edge. This helps to keep their wrists in a neutral position for accuracy.
  - "Open, shut them" helps with pacing. Many children will make one snip and stop, but it takes practice and support to continually cut with multiple snips.

Sit in a chair behind a child, and have them sit or stand in front of you. This will make it easier to demonstrate the steps to children who need it, especially if you need to use hand-over-hand support to help them open and close the scissors while you provide pacing and verbal encouragement.

Case Study: Helping Jaime Successfully Use Scissors

Your classroom has several pairs of blunt-tipped preschool scissors. The activity for the day is to cut out small squares with animal pictures on them and glue them onto a worksheet. Jaime picks up the scissors, places one hand on each loop, and tries to snip the paper by opening and closing the scissors. What should you do?

Jaime's unfamiliarity with scissors is obvious, as he holds each of the handles in a different hand. He is definitely going to need some help to cut out those squares on his own. You have a few choices to help him be successful:

- Quickly pre-cut the paper, cutting out most of the blocks and leaving just the straight lines between two blocks, so that he only needs to snip the straight lines.

- Reposition Jaime's fingers into the blunt-tipped scissors, with his thumb in the top opening, his index finger in the second opening, and his middle finger resting underneath the hinge. Offer verbal cues to open and close the scissors while helping him cut out the items.
- Offer alternative scissors (if possible), such as loop scissors or hinged scissors. Help him hold the scissors in a thumbs-up position, and use hand-over-hand support to squeeze the scissors to help him be successful. After a few tries of helping him, fade away your cues and encourage him to squeeze the scissors on his own.

A few weeks later, Jaime has made great progress with his scissor skills. He knows how to put the scissor openings on his hands, can make a few snips, and is now trying to cut along a line. This time, when you give him a similar activity in which he needs to cut along a straight line, he picks up the scissors in his right hand, holds the paper in his left, and tries to cut horizontally across the paper. Now what should you do?

- Check Jaime's grasp pattern to make sure his hands are in the correct openings and his index finger is under the hinge. Does he need a pair of looped or hinged scissors to make it easier, or is he doing okay with adjusting his grip on the blunt-tipped scissors?
- Turn the paper so the line he is cutting is in a vertical position.
- Demonstrate to Jaime the concept of "stable on the table" and remind him that his elbow should be at his side or on the table so he can cut with his thumbs pointing up. Give him a chance to cut the line from the bottom of the line to the top, and give him a ton of positive encouragement along the way.

Using the Right Paper

I bet you never thought that the paper you use for cutting could make a huge difference in a child's success in using scissors. Most children (and adults) are familiar with standard copy paper. Using different types and sizes of paper, however, can help achieve different outcomes.

Construction paper is less flimsy than copy paper, and card stock is even thicker than construction paper. Thicker paper is more challenging to cut when children have weaker hand strength and less control. For children with well-developed hand strength and control, thicker paper is actually easier to cut, because it's easier to grip and encourages consistent use of both hands. One hand can focus on positioning the paper while the other hand operates the scissors to cut. Also consider the size of the paper and the thickness of the lines printed on it, as well as the overall size of the shapes the children are cutting out. If you would like the children to cut out a small shape, pre-cut around it to offer them less paper in general, so it's easier to cut.

Finding Scissor Cutting Activities

You can find many printable cutting activities online, both free and for a small fee, from various websites (see the textbox below for website information).

For a fun activity to help children shift their paper with their nondominant hand, search for printables by using the keywords "thumbprint cutting strips." These printables include a marked spot for placing the thumb, which helps in coordinating hand movements and stabilizing the paper while cutting, especially when maneuvering around curves and edges with scissors. If you find thumbprint cutting strips, make sure you have both the right- and left-handed versions to accommodate children who are lefties, too. You'll find many themed cutting strips and puzzles to print. Using cutting activities that are based around an upcoming holiday, a theme, or a child's interests will definitely improve their motivation. Children can find cutting to be a real challenge in the beginning until they have some confidence.

Websites with Printables

Many sites have printables that can be downloaded and used to build strength, coordination, scissor cutting skills, and writing skills. While some printables are free, others can be downloaded for small fees. Here are some websites to check out:

- **EdHelper** https://www.edhelper.com/preschool.htm
- **Educational Insights** https://www.educationalinsights.com/sparkmoreplay
- **Fun365** https://www.fun365.orientaltrading.com/classroom-ideas
- **Hand2Mind** https://www.hand2mind.com/lessons
- **Lakeshore Learning** https://www.lakeshorelearning.com/resources/free-resources
- **Learning Resources** https://learningresources.com
- **LessonPix** https://lessonpix.com
- **OTPlan** https://otplan.com/select-material (Search by material to find related activities.)
- **PBS LearningMedia** https://kera.pbslearningmedia.org
- **Pre-K Pages** https://www.pre-kpages.com
- **Super Teacher Worksheets** https://www.superteacherworksheets.com
- **TeAch-nology** https://www.teach-nology.com

- **The OT Toolbox** https://www.theottoolbox.com
- **Therapy Fun Zone** https://therapyfunzone.net/blog
- **Therapy Materials Vault** https://therapymaterialsvault.com
- **Teachers Pay Teachers** https://www.teacherspayteachers.com
- **Tools to Grow** https://www.toolstogrowot.com
- **Your Therapy Source** https://www.yourtherapysource.com

Now that you know how to properly choose scissors based on a child's age and skill level and how to modify scissor activities to offer children success, you'll find it rewarding to see each child's confidence with scissors develop. Next, let's move on to one of the most challenging early childhood visual motor skills: handwriting.

CHAPTER 9:

Moving Up the Skill Ladder: Beginning Writing

At the same time children are learning to use scissors, scribble, and color, they are also learning how to draw, copy line designs, and write letters. Children develop these skills as their visual motor skills progress. In this chapter, we look at the development process for pencil-and-paper activities, which includes a specific progression of skills required to learn to draw pictures and to write upper- and lowercase letters, children's names, and eventually sentences to create a story.

Pre-Writing Strokes

It's important to know the kinds of drawing and writing skills children typically have at different ages. This understanding will help you have realistic expectations for how well they can color, draw, and write. Many people don't realize that if you ask a child to draw something that is too hard for their age, they might not do it at all. Instead, children will often pick something more fun that they prefer to do.

Occupational therapists use standardized testing to determine where a child is developmentally in terms of writing readiness. A popular tool is the *Beery-Buktenica Developmental Test of Visual-Motor Integration* (Beery, Buktenica, and Beery, 2010). Here is the developmental progression of writing strokes by age as described in this tool.

Vertical line . . . . 2 years

Horizontal line . . . . 2½ years

Circle . . . . 3 years

Cross. . . . . 3½–4 years

Square . . . . 4 years

Right oblique diagonal line (/). . . . . 4½ years

Left oblique diagonal line (\) . . . . . . 4½ years

X, or oblique cross. . . . . 4 years, 11 months

Triangle . . . . 5 years

This means that for children to form complicated letters of the alphabet, they generally need to be able to imitate and copy an adult making these specific lines or shapes. In the next section, we look at how these developmental ages of pre-writing strokes apply to children's coloring, drawing, and writing letters of the alphabet.

Coloring

Coloring and drawing are important skills, not just for school or as activities families offer their children to pass the time on airplanes or car trips, in a restaurant, or on a rainy day.

A two-year-old will most likely pick up a crayon using a fisted grasp or pronated grasp pattern and draw different types of random marks and scribbles on the paper. They might not yet have mastered the art of coloring and definitely not of coloring within the lines. At two and a half, they usually can make vertical and horizontal scribbles.

A three-year-old might show some variation in their grasp patterns, depending upon their exposure, experience, and developmental level. Some children might start coloring activities with a static tripod grasp pattern and, when they get tired, switch back to a pronated grasp pattern that is generally seen with younger children. Overall, however, three-year-olds should be showing more control to use their fingers to hold writing utensils. They can create clearly formed vertical lines and horizontal lines and can change direction while drawing to create a circle, even forming it so that the ends close.

A four-year-old should pick up a crayon with a mature dynamic tripod grasp pattern and be able to focus on coloring in some of the shapes printed on a page. Most likely, they will not quite keep the crayon within the lines; instead, they might make large, sweeping motions with their crayon over the picture. Children at this age can make vertical lines, horizontal lines, and circular motions, which can be incorporated into their coloring projects.

So how do you help children make the transition to paying attention to detail when coloring?

Color with them and engage them with you in the process. Children benefit from being shown exactly how something needs to be done, so they can use that demonstration as a reference. For example, if you are coloring a picture of a puppy, pick up any color crayon and ask what body part the child would like to color on the dog: "Oh, the nose? Okay." Then, outline the nose with your crayon and show them how to color within the lines. Ask which body part, letter, or feature they'd like to color next, and outline it for them. Then, hand the crayon over for them to try, encouraging them to imitate how you colored within the lines earlier.

Show them how to color using the small motions of their fingers, as many children who don't have the proper strength in their hands yet will make larger motions using the elbow, wrist, and so on. Pick out smaller shapes for children to color, and give them a bold, defined boundary. This can help children visually focus on the small details. Attention plays an important role in visual motor skills when accuracy is needed. Sometimes, giving children a smaller shape to color helps them visually focus on the small details and improves their control.

When demonstrating this process, don't stop coloring right away; really invest yourself in the activity. So much of teaching children these skills is setting aside a little time to model and perform. Children learn through repetition after repeated demonstrations. Showing them how you color will help to remind them what the expectations are.

For children who are challenged with staying in the lines, there are a few other fun activities you can try:

- Outline the border of the shape with puffy paint, and let it dry before asking children to color it in. The bumpy edge helps offer a tactile cue to remind children of how to stay inside the shape.
- Use Wikki Stix. These colorful, wax-covered pieces of string are moldable and bendable; lots of children use them to make creations. Place the strips on the borders of shapes or pictures before children color inside them, and then remove the Wikki Stix after coloring.

Case Study: Helping Marisol Improve Her Accuracy in Coloring

Marisol is five years old. You give her a coloring sheet, and she picks up a standard, thin crayon and attempts to scribble and color with her hand in a pronated grasp pattern. She makes large marks on the paper without paying attention to the lines. What can you do to help develop her grasp and improve her accuracy for coloring?

If you have standard, thin crayons, a simple fix is to just break them in half. Sometimes, having access to only a small portion of the crayon reduces the temptation to pick it up and hold it with the whole hand, allowing for more control with the fingertips.

To help Marisol color within the lines, use a crayon or a marker to outline one of the shapes on the page—maybe a specific detail. Then, encourage her to use her crayon to color within the area that you outlined. Using hand-over-hand support can help her understand staying within the boundaries. Then, ask her which shape she'd like to color next, outline it, and encourage her to color within the lines just like she did when you helped her.

Tracing

Tracing is when a child uses their finger or a writing tool to closely follow or draw on a line. Many children like to draw a line through a path or a defined area like a maze.

Tracing paths of varying widths can help children develop their eye-hand coordination and control using a marker or pencil. Start with wide, straight paths, and then make them smaller as children's skills improve. Add bends and curves to change direction. Highlighters are a fun tool to make simple paths and mazes on plain paper.

You can also find inexpensive dot-to-dot and maze books at dollar stores or print them from the internet. I often create my own age-appropriate paths and mazes for children using a whiteboard and dry-erase markers. Children's favorite reusable decals and stickers also stick well to whiteboards and can be connected with markers through paths.

While tracing letters can be helpful, make sure that children trace using proper formation. Later in this chapter, we will consider curriculums that can be used to teach letter formation and use a top-to-bottom approach with a specific sequence of lines. At young ages, some children will pick up a marker, place it on a line, and randomly move along the line without any specific order. This is often seen when children in preschool are learning to write letters of the alphabet. While this is developmentally expected, if they use this approach frequently and aren't actually learning the formation, they might develop bad habits that can affect their letter formation later on.

One popular strategy is to make dotted lines in the form of a letter and encourage children to trace from one dot to another. This strategy, however, is not generally helpful in memory for letter formation. Many children just see a lot of dots on the page and will start connecting them in any order they choose. Skip the dotted lines altogether. Instead, try using a yellow highlighter to make the shape in a fluid line, and then provide the child with a starting dot at the top. If using this method when helping a child learn to write letters, take turns making each letter. Don't just write their name in highlighter across the page and hand over a marker. Demonstrate making the letter with the highlighter, give them a starting dot at the beginning of that letter, then allow them to trace inside the highlighted path on their own with a marker or pencil. After that letter is complete, start the process again with another letter. You write the letter with the highlighter, and then they write it with a marker inside the highlighted path.

Case Study: Helping Usha Trace with Accuracy

A kindergarten class is working on tracing and then writing the letters of their names. Usha picks up a pencil and holds it in the middle of the shaft, using her entire fist in a palmar grasp. She pushes so hard on the paper that the pencil tip breaks. What can you do to help her hold the pencil better and then trace with accuracy?

A palmar grasp pattern in kindergarten can pose a bit of a challenge for students who are trying to perform more accurate activities, such as tracing letters. You could swap Usha's pencil for a thicker, shorter marker. Adding a vertical or slanted surface, such as a three-ring binder, under the paper can help raise it off the tabletop, which would encourage Usha's fingers to come together in a fingertip grasp pattern.

If you don't swap out her pencil, in this case, given that she is in kindergarten, I would consider adding a pencil grip—either the Pencil Grip or the Grotto grip options—to her pencil to help Usha learn proper finger placement. We'll talk more about pencil grips later in this chapter.

In terms of helping to improve her control when tracing, use a highlighter to trace over and form the letters, starting from the top to the bottom, to model the proper formation. Encourage her to use either her marker or the pencil with the grip to imitate the strokes you made, working inside the highlighted lines.

Drawing People and Other Objects

Three-year-olds, who can typically draw vertical, horizontal, and circular lines, often begin experimenting with drawing a face. Next, the arms and legs (vertical and horizontal lines) will emerge from a circular shape.

At four and a half to five years of age, children can draw a person with multiple and recognizable body parts. As they learn to recreate a cross, square, and triangle, many children can incorporate these shapes into simple representational drawings of items such as a house or a train.

Step-by-step drawing is really helpful at the early childhood level, showing children how to integrate and copy complicated shapes in a structured but fun way that has nothing to do with letters.

Mat Man

Mat Man is a popular concept used to teach children how to draw a person. It was developed by Jan Olsen, a pediatric occupational therapist who designed the Handwriting Without Tears program (now known as Learning Without Tears). This program helps teach children letter formation by first incorporating manipulatives and teaching spatial concepts. Mat Man has become a well-known part of the curriculum, and many children learn to draw a person using this method.

Using a song, book, and large wooden pieces, with the addition of a few smaller shapes that can be recreated from a template, children first learn to assemble an image of a person with these items. Once they learn about their body parts and how to make the person, the idea is easily generalized to paper with a marker or crayon.

Organized by grade level, Learning Without Tears is a developmentally based curriculum that teaches young children about spatial awareness and letter formation. Many schools have adopted this curriculum at the early childhood level, and OTs are also familiar with the principles of the curriculum to help children with special needs learn letter formation. To learn more about it, see the website (https://www.lwtears.com).

Using Pencil Grips

At the kindergarten and early elementary level, you can offer pencil grips as an option to help children improve their grasp patterns if they are being asked to do a lot of writing and their grasp patterns are affecting their performance. For example, if, despite remediation efforts, a child continues to use an inefficient grasp pattern such as a thumb-wrap or fisted grasp, the grasp pattern will often make it difficult to write letters in small spaces with the right pressure. Pencil grips can be used with children whether they are right- or left-handed. Even in the elementary years, it's important to continue to build strength and coordination for a more mature grasp pattern when possible.

For preschool-aged children, modifying writing tools and teaching proper grasp patterns should be the first line of defense. Generally, shorter, fatter utensils, such as Crayola Pip Squeak markers, broken standard crayons, mini-golf pencils, or triangular markers, are great alternatives. Preschool-aged children should not be using standard-length pencils at all.

Types of Pencil Grips

While pencil grips should be reserved for use with children at the kindergarten level and early elementary levels, I list some of the popular options in case you need them.

- **Rubber bands:** A rubber band is a low-tech, simple way to remind children to hold their pencils in the correct spot near the tip. Wind a rubber band around the pencil near the tip, right where the paint meets the sharpened part. Some children just need this as a subtle cue for where to place their fingers.
- **Comfort grips:** These are squishy, bumpy, foam-type grips that are attached slightly above the tip of the pencil and offer a little more input than an elastic band.
- **Triangular grips:** Some companies make triangular-shaped crayons, markers, and pencils, but if you have standard pencils, you can also get a triangular-shaped grip to add to a pencil. This grip helps to increase the width of the pencil, making it easier to grasp.
- **Pencil Grip:** This design might be one of the most common pencil grips; it has been available for decades. Its ergonomic shape is cushioned, making it more comfortable for children to have a specific spot to rest their thumb and index and middle fingers in the correct placement. A larger Pencil Grip also helps children who use excessive writing pressure or are not writing using dynamic movements, such as maneuvering the pencil with their thumb and index and middle fingers.
- **Grotto Grip:** The Grotto Grip is a large, sturdy grip with very specific places for the child to position their thumb and index and middle fingers. Children can position their fingers inside the grip because a lip around the edge helps them keep their fingers in place. The Grotto Grip is helpful in redirecting a stubborn thumb-wrap grip or multifinger grasp pattern.

- **Pencil weights:** These help children who have decreased awareness or low muscle tone to hold a pencil. They are also effective for children who have a light grasp to write darker. Using pencil weights can position the pencil in the correct location of the web space of the hand, prompting a more effective grasp.
- **HandiWriter:** The HandiWriter is a soft loop worn on the wrist or forearm. The pencil is attached through a small loop above the wrist, and the child holds the pencil with their fingers. A small charm on a ribbon is also attached to the HandiWriter, so that children can hold the charm underneath the ring and pinky fingers, promoting a tripod-style grasp pattern. The tension from the elastic helps to position the pencil in the web space and offers a more optimal grip. Don't want to buy a HandiWriter? Use a soft hair elastic around the wrist. Twist the elastic to create a loop for the pencil, then have the child hold a pompom in their ring and pinky fingers.

Letter Writing and Formation

After children have progressed from prewriting strokes to coloring and then to tracing and drawing, they are ready to learn the next skill: how to write letters. This section provides strategies for helping you teach children this important skill.

Start with Wake-Up Activities

Rather than jumping right into instruction for writing, wake up the muscles in the hand. The following activities help children become aware of their muscles and hands and build the strength needed to hold pencils. Check out the section about hand strength and pinch strength in chapter 4 for even more activities to try.

- Manipulate fidgets and windup toys
- Squish stress balls
- Push buttons on pop-up toys
- Knead and flatten putty
- Roll toys in the fingertips
- Use tongs to pick up small toys and place them in a container

Offer Slanted Surfaces

Incorporating vertical surfaces, such as art easels, can help children build proper grip and control as they naturally put the wrist into extension. When the wrist is extended, the fingers tend to naturally come together in a fingertip grasp pattern. Placing worksheets and doing paint projects on stand-up or wall-mounted easels, whiteboards, and chalkboards can offer a different way to work that helps promote fine motor skills. I do not recommend using tabletop easels, as these tend to be less stable than those that rest on the floor. If you need a tabletop solution, get a large two- or three-inch three-ring binder and turn it horizontally (so that the spine is farthest from the child) to create a sloped surface. Some people mount clipboards to binders using Velcro. If the binder has a sleeve in the front to hold a piece of paper, inserting a worksheet there and using a dry-erase marker can make the worksheet reusable.

Many teachers make photocopies of letter-formation worksheets, mazes, and other pencil-and-paper activities and slip them into sheet protectors. These can be housed inside a binder, then removed and placed on the slanted surface. Using a dry-erase marker on these sheet protectors can also make the papers reusable.

Use a Developmentally Appropriate Handwriting Curriculum

Many preschool centers and programs feel pressured to show families that they are preparing children academically for school, often by focusing on tangible results such as how quickly they can teach young children to write their names. Jumping to pencil-and-paper worksheets is often the first step for programs, but it's not the best choice. Most preschool-aged children are not developmentally ready to control a pencil to write. Offering activities that are too challenging too soon can also lead to poor habits. Sometimes, children will show behaviors such as avoiding activities, not getting started, or becoming easily frustrated.

Finding fun ways to learn about identifying letters through games and activities is a better approach. If you are not sure where to start, begin with handwriting curriculums designed for younger children, offering workshops and well-researched activities that are appropriate for specific age groups. Curriculums such as Learning Without Tears are built on supporting important fine motor skills and include easy-to-remember verbal scripts to use when teaching.

Teach uppercase letter formation before lowercase formation. Uppercase is developmentally easier for young children because the letters require larger, simpler strokes. Lowercase letter formations have more complicated shapes that require more skill; teaching them too soon can lead to habits that are challenging to fix. For example, when children are forming a lowercase letter *b*, they are taught to start at the top, make a straight line down, come up slightly on the same straight line, then curve it around to the base of the tall line, all in one stroke without lifting the pencil. Children who aren't developmentally ready to form these letters aren't capable of performing all those steps. To finish the task, they make a straight vertical line from the bottom to the top, lift their pencil, and make a circle at the base of the line. Looks like a lowercase *b*, right? Over time, however, practicing segmented letter formation makes writing sentences difficult and inefficient, which can lead to fatigue.

Handwriting Curricula

Not sure how to go about teaching handwriting? Here are some popular curricula to choose from that have been specifically designed for early childhood classrooms and have structured lesson plans to follow.

- D'Nealian Handwriting https://www.savvas.com/index.cfm?locator=PS3gMv
- Learning Without Tears https://www.lwtears.com
- Zaner-Bloser Handwriting https://shop.zaner-bloser.com

Kindergarten readiness is a huge part of preschool. Learning about handwriting curriculums, rather than simply downloading or creating worksheets, will give you the step-by-step activities you need and will save you from a lot of frustration.

Letter-Identification Activities

Before you jump into encouraging children to start with writing letters, teach the children what letters are and how to identify them. This can be done through multisensory motor activities that don't involve any writing at all. Provide a variety of fun activities that help children develop letter awareness and identification. Here are some of my favorites:

- **Alphabet beach ball:** Write some or all letters of the alphabet on a beach ball. Invite the children to toss it around, choose a letter, and find a corresponding matching letter on a card, on a poster, or from a pile of letter manipulatives.
- **Letter hide-and-seek:** Hide letters around the room. Then, give each child a letter card, and ask them to find and bring back the matching letter.
- **Letter skywriting:** Have children write letters in the air with their hands. Using large muscle movements involves kinesthesia, which will help children remember the formation of letters as they learn by doing.

- **Letter grab:** Place alphabet beanbags or alphabet letters on the floor. Show a child a letter card and invite the child to find and bring back the matching letter by using lots of different gross motor actions, such as sliding on a scooter board, jumping like a frog, hopping on one foot, or crawling on their hands and feet. This is a good way to build strength and improve attention and focus while tackling letter identification.

A variety of games and toys can support fine motor skills as well as letter identification:

- Puzzles (form boards and self-correcting letter-matching puzzles)
- Magnetic letter fishing games
- Snap-n-Learn alphabet toys by Learning Resources
- Letter Snap Blocks by Unifix
- Magnetic letters on a cookie sheet
- Alphabet nuts and bolts
- Alphabet bingo
- Boggle Jr. by Hasbro
- Zingo! by ThinkFun
- Alphabet beads and chenille stems by Kaplan Early Learning
- Letter stamps
- Alphabet beanbags
- Alphabet Pebbles by Kaplan Early Learning

Fine Motor Sensory Activities to Build Letter Awareness

While we certainly have many flashcard options to build letter identification and awareness, a better choice includes using sensory mediums paired with letters and other toys. Sensory activities tend to engage children for longer periods—they love to learn by doing.

First, print and laminate alphabet picture cards on card stock. Then, choose a sensory medium from the list below, and use the sensory medium to recreate the letter. The children can use their hands to roll, shape, squeeze, and form letters with that medium, developing the foundational skills for formation while also building awareness. Here are some fun sensory mediums and activities to try:

- Wikki Stix
- Do-a-Dot markers
- Sandpaper
- Playfoam
- Playdough

- Kinetic Sand
- Gluing tissue paper or paper scraps onto printed letter sheets
- Placing stickers onto printed letter sheets
- Wood Pieces Set for Capital Letters and Capital Letter Cards by Learning Without Tears

Tracing and Formation Activities

Once children gain an understanding of what letters are and how to recognize them, they can begin to do tracing and formation activities. The following are some activities to support letter tracing and formation:

- Sandpaper letters and textured tracing cards
- Shaving-cream tracing
- Magnetic stylus activities, such as Magnatabs
- Stencils
- Wet-Dry-Try method from Learning Without Tears, which uses a wet sponge, chalk, and a chalkboard
- Letter apps using a stylus, such as the following:
  - Writing Wizard
  - iWriteWords
  - Get Set for School by Learning Without Tears

Learning Without Tears suggests a top-to-bottom approach for letter formation while writing across the page from left to right. I recommend monitoring children with these kinds of activities so that formation is modeled correctly in the beginning and can be solidified into children's mindsets over time.

Pencil-and-Paper Writing Activities

Once children begin writing letters, there are some considerations to keep in mind to set them up for success:

- Make sure the chair and table heights in your classroom are appropriate for the children's ages.

- Provide children with pencils, markers, crayons, and scissors that are recommended for their ages.
- If a child is beginning to write their name and is in preschool, provide them with a laminated version of their name on lined paper. Putting a sticker or colored dot at the top line can help remind children where the starting point is. Laminated name tags can be used for tracing activities with a dry-erase marker, then easily wiped clean.
- Try rainbow writing, which is tracing a letter in the correct order in different colors according to the sequence of the rainbow (red, orange, yellow, green, blue, indigo, violet). It's a great kinesthetic activity to create motor memory, but it should be monitored to make sure children are tracing and copying in the proper directions.
- For circular letters, such as *O,* that start in the middle and move left to form the letter, place a dot with a little line from the dot to the left to help children get started in forming the circle in the correct direction.
- If you decide to offer worksheets, keep them short. You can cut worksheets into smaller pieces to avoid overwhelming young children.
- The type of paper you choose is important. Large pieces of white paper without lines or structure make writing difficult. Children will often randomly write letters in any order, anywhere on the page. Instead, use horizontal strips of paper, as they naturally help with letter sizing.
    - Dotted, lined paper is helpful for children who are beginning to write letters, words, phrases, and sentences.
    - To help with letter sizing, consider using paper that has baselines that are highlighted yellow.
    - Paper with raised, bumpy lines can assist with letter sizing and line boundaries.

★ ★ ★

We've discussed many ways to help children improve their visual motor skills. There are so many other creative activities to do to help advance a child's fine motor skills. Many classrooms and families are incorporating technology, in moderation, into their daily activities. For those who plan to include tablets and apps in the classroom, in the next chapter I'll share some of my favorite choices.

CHAPTER 10:
Using Technology to Promote Visual Motor Skills

In the previous chapters, we explored activities using hands-on materials to support children's fine motor and visual motor skills. But what about technology? Technology, for better or worse, is a significant part of a young child's life. In my opinion, it's important to prioritize fun games and activities, using technology more as a supplementary tool. However, some children may be most motivated by technology. In this chapter, we cover ways to incorporate technology in the classroom, primarily by sharing some general considerations on what to expect when using apps. I highlight some well-developed apps that appropriately promote fine motor skills, and I offer information how to position a child when using an app and whether to use a stylus.

Before You Get Started

For five years, I wrote reviews for educational apps and websites for Common Sense Media; I have reviewed a lot of technology. Here's some helpful information to know before using technology, particularly apps, in the classroom or at home:

- **App fee structures differ widely.** Some apps include a one-time fee to buy them forever. Others have a recurring subscription fee that is charged monthly unless you cancel. Many apps are free to download but ask you to pay for activities, upgrades, or special features as you go. These are known as "in-app purchases" and can have different prices. Be advised that many free apps often include advertisements, which can distract children from learning. Consider setting aside a small budget to purchase a few apps so that children can engage with appropriate content rather than being exposed to content that might detract from learning.

- **Apps can be shared across devices.** Purchasing an app once allows you to download it and use it on multiple devices simultaneously. Note that some apps might work only on tablets and not on smartphones. Searching the app store on the device or devices you plan to use for these apps will help you find the most compatible ones.
- **Tablets are generally better than phones.** When possible, install apps on tablets. Tablets provide a bigger space for children to use their fine motor skills as well as a larger surface on which to see smaller details.
- **Apps that include offline play offer flexibility.** This is important in case you need to use an app offline when a device is not connected to Wi-Fi.

Once you install an app, keep it updated. Apps can get bugs or have glitches and stop working without warning. Regularly completing app updates will increase the chances of success when using them. Older apps that are no longer supported with updates might not be compatible with newer devices. And newer apps might not be able to be used with older devices that cannot update to the latest operating systems. Always check your device's specifications against an app's requirements before buying.

Get to know your device's settings. Many devices include customization options that allow you to turn sound on and off, increase the size of items on the screen, and so forth. These allow you to personalize activities for each child's current skill level. Many apps also track usage and data, so I recommend viewing the developer's privacy policy for each app. Ideally, sitting with children to offer feedback, tech support, and guidance will help them stay on track and be less distracted when they use an app.

Consider using additional control apps on devices. There are subscriptions to apps such as OurPact, Net Nanny, and FamilyTime that will allow you to control several devices at once. With the click of a button on your personal device, you can shut off access to an entire device or to certain apps. This offers a lot more control than the parental controls often included on individual devices. These apps are not inexpensive, but they can prevent you from having to physically take a device out of the hands of a child who isn't transitioning away from the device or respecting a time limit. Schedules can also be put into place to limit the use of certain apps to certain times of the day, which lets family members and teachers monitor screen-time activities.

Protecting Devices

Children will probably drop the devices a lot, and the screens can crack easily, which will lead to expensive repairs. Considering a warranty when buying electronic devices that will be used by children is always a good idea. Invest in some durable cases, such as the LTROP Kids Case, available on Amazon.com. Before ordering, check to make sure that the cases you are considering are designed for the specific devices you use. When searching for a child-friendly case, look for one with an integrated stand and handles that make it easy for children to carry the device.

Using Devices

How a device is positioned during use makes a difference. When tablets are flat, children tend to hunch over them and flex their necks, which could lead to neck pain and poor posture over time. Viewing content with the tablet in an upright position will encourage children to sit up taller and let them see the screen with less neck strain. When playing games on a device, adjusting the position to have a partial slant is perfect. Using it in this position encourages slight extension of the wrist and leads to a preferred grasp pattern. Need a way to help stand up a phone? PopSockets are a useful tool for smaller devices.

What About a Stylus?

Many devices allow the user to trace with a single finger to control an app. Many children, however, use both thumbs when texting or playing a video game, which can lead to poor habits that affect hand-muscle development. Styluses are an excellent option, especially if children are using their devices with apps designed for tracing and forming letters and numbers. A stylus is like a pen but has a soft rubber end that is safe to use on device screens. Examples such as the Youth Series Kids Stylus Pen by Fosman and the Kids Stylus Pens for Touch Screens by StylusHome (both available on Amazon.com) are excellent options. They are made of durable rubber, so they are safe to use on screens, and their thicker-width design promotes a more functional grip for younger children.

Case Study: Using Tablets for Letter Formation

You received a grant that brought tablets into your classroom. How can you effectively use these devices to help children with letter formation?

First, physically set up the tablets in a vertical or slanted position, using the handles on the covers to prop them up. Consider downloading apps such as iWriteWords or Writing Wizard and offering children the use of a stylus when they are tracing. Start with simple lines or uppercase letters first, then progress to smaller, curved letters in lowercase formation.

Make sure to set expectations on how long to use the tablets. Consider the use of a monitoring app such as OurPact and, if needed, have all the devices turn off after a predetermined amount of time, such as ten minutes of use. To reduce frustration, warn children of the remaining time and the upcoming transition, and plan something fun and exciting to do next, such as heading out for recess or taking a classroom brain break.

Apps for Supporting Fine Motor and Visual Motor Skills

As I noted earlier in this chapter, I've reviewed many apps. Here is a suggested list of popular apps to improve fine motor and visual spatial skills. While prices are not listed, be mindful that many apps include a one-time fee to buy or a recurring subscription fee per month. Others may be free to download but ask you to pay for activities with in-app purchases. Items indicated by an asterisk(*) can be used on an Android tablet with the Google Play store or on a Kindle Fire that has access to the Amazon Appstore.

Fine Motor Apps

Bugs and Bundle
- Bugs and Bubbles
- Bugs and Numbers
- Bugs and Beyond
- Bug Art
- Bug Mazing

Dexteria Dots*

Dexteria Jr.*

Endless Learning Academy (2–5)*
- Endless Alphabet
- Endless Numbers
- Endless Wordplay
- Endless Reader

Highlights Hidden Pictures*

Highlights Shapes*

iTrace

iWriteWords

Jolly Phonics Lessons

Lego Duplo World*

LetterSchool*

Osmo World*

PBS Kids Games*

Pinkfong*
- Pinkfong Tracing World
- Pinkfong My Body
- Pinkfong Shapes & Colors
- Baby Shark ABC Phonics
- Baby Shark Coloring Book
- Baby Shark Jigsaw Puzzle Fun
- Pinkfong Spot the Difference

Ready to Print*

Trace It Try It

Touch and Write

Wet-Dry-Try Handwriting

Writing Wizard for Kids, school edition*

Self-Care Apps

Baby Shark Wash Your Hands*

Choiceworks

Habitica *

Pepi Bath & Pepi Bath 2*

Pinkfong My Body*

Educational Game Systems for Tablets

Many people know that apps can be downloaded to tablets, but fewer know about the excellent educational systems specifically designed for tablets that take learning to a different level. Educational systems like these are bought in kits and usually designed around an academic topic, such as reading, math, or coding. Some systems focus on science, technology, engineering, and math (STEM). Unlike traditional apps, these kits have manipulatives, which encourage learning with small pieces such as letters, shapes, and numbers that can be aligned, rotated, and connected. These systems use digital learning through apps but combine it with unique pieces that build fine motor skills, too. Here are some educational game systems to consider.

Osmo is a system that operates on a tablet as well as the accompanying pieces. Set the tablet in the base, and position a reflector on top over the camera. This allows the device to communicate with the manipulatives from the kit. The app prompts children to draw pictures, align shapes to create letters, or spell words with letter tiles, and then gives immediate feedback on their performance. The curriculum is designed for specific age groups and gets progressively harder as children learn new skills. It's an excellent way to promote learning along with fine motor skills at the same time.

PlayShifu is a tablet-based, augmented-reality educational program. Children learn concepts, solve puzzles, and engage in challenges by placing different manipulatives on top of the tablet screen. Large pieces promote the use of a fingertip grasp pattern as children tap, rotate, and slide manipulatives to play interactive board games and activities.

Boom Cards

Boom cards are digital task cards that allow the user to connect to online games and activities. These can be played on a computer, tablet, or smartphone with internet access. The website I prefer using is BoomLearning.com, which is where teachers, OTs, speech therapists, and special educators can create decks of virtual cards to sell in an online store on the website. These interactive activities are often focused on a theme or learning concept, such as phonics, letters, math, or self-care skills such as washing hands and using the toilet. Teachers Pay Teachers (Teacherspayteachers.com) also has boom-card options.

Once loaded, the activities often include sorting games and step-by-step sequences that children can complete using a mouse or touch screen. What makes boom cards unique is that once a child completes the task on an individual card, they hit "submit" and the program will let them know if they were correct or incorrect in their choice. Some of the "decks" of cards are free, but others must be purchased. They can range in price, but I have found many free options that are excellent for the early childhood age group. Lots of teachers create their own interactive, educational boom cards; the library of activities is extensive. You can easily search by grade or content area. These games are also fun when played by an individual child with a stylus to work on eye-hand coordination on the screen. Boom cards are easily adapted to use in small groups for targeted instruction, too.

Case Study: Learning Handwashing Skills

Presleigh, a three-year-old girl in the early childhood classroom, is always quick to wash her hands after using the bathroom. However, she never remembers to use soap and is unable to motor plan how to get the soap out of the container. Instead, she turns on the water, wets her hands, turns off the water, and leaves the bathroom with her hands soaking wet. When you try to demonstrate how to dry her hands, she's already across the classroom waiting for you to open the technology cart and does not seem interested in learning the steps. How can you help Presleigh improve her fine motor skills to wash her hands more thoroughly if she's not interested in doing the steps?

Presleigh appears to be motivated by technology. During planning time, you can log into BoomLearning.com and search the decks in the store for "handwashing." Filter the price range and scroll thorough the dozens of options. The decks to choose from include games, step-by-step instructions, and sequences. Some have real photos; others have animated drawings. Pick a few free options, add them to your library, and spend a few minutes testing them.

If Presleigh isn't the only child who could use a little more help remembering the handwashing steps, you can create a small group later in the week with Presleigh and a few other children. Gather them, grab a tablet, go to the internet, log in to Boom Learning, and load the "Wash Your Hands! Sequence Steps" by Tools to Grow. This particular deck includes step-by step interactive instructions. Ask a child to help you by using their finger to drag the correct icon for step 1, which is, "Do we dry or wash hands first?" Let the child submit her choices for each step, taking turns to let other children submit their choices.

After the center, to reinforce what the students have learned, print the last slide, laminate it, and post it by the sink as a visual reminder of the steps. The next week, you might notice that Presleigh is still not as thorough, but at least she is now completing all the steps and is no longer running around with wet hands after using the bathroom.

I hope you will give boom cards a try. They are something a little different to inspire those children who are motivated by interactive activities.

★ ★ ★

One of the best ways for children to make progress is to have a community of teachers, family members, and therapists who are committed to their success. In the last chapter, I highlight some ways to help families get involved with fine motor activities to help your students get exposure at home, so you can all work on the classroom goals and objectives together.

CHAPTER 11:

Ways to Help Families Promote Fine Motor Skills at Home

Now that you are armed with lots of strategies and activities to help children develop their fine motor skills, you'll want to get families on board as well. As with any new skill, children need to practice throughout the day—both at school and at home. Offer families some suggestions on ways they can easily reinforce learning at home.

Use your program's newsletter to communicate with families about what's happening during class each week. Include specific links to videos, printables, and websites the children have used in their activities. Children love to be in charge of "teaching" their family members, and reinforcing classroom learning at home offers more opportunities for them to learn through practice and repetition. So many families tell me how frustrated they get when they ask their child about their day and don't get any relevant information. This is a great way for families to connect with their children.

Engage in Arts-and-Crafts Activities

Arts-and-crafts activities can be a helpful way to support fine motor skills. But organizing these activities can take families, especially those who aren't crafty, a lot of time to gather and organize materials and figure out what to do with them. Consider sending home simple premade craft kits to make it easy to inspire families to get involved. Dollar stores often have packages of simple crafts that include sticker activities to create a themed item. Many products include six copies of the same activity per package. So, for just a few dollars, children can take home a premade craft they should be able to do with little supervision while waiting for a sibling at a sports practice or waiting for a family member to make dinner. If you have an abundance of leftover materials such as googly eyes, cotton balls, scrap paper, ribbons, and stickers, package some in a ziplock bag and send those home too. Encourage family members to see what their children can create with the materials. Consider encouraging the children to take photos to show you what they made or to bring their creations back to school, where you can feature them in a classroom display. This might help offer some motivation for children to engage in using their fine motor skills more confidently at home.

Provide Families with Activity Lists

Aside from arts-and-crafts, sending home activity lists of toys to play with and games to try is also helpful to transfer learning to home. For example, many children already have common toys, bubbles, markers, blocks, or stuffed animals. Kitchen-tool drawers often have tongs, spoons, and small cups.

Appendix C lists common items that you can use as inspiration to create some fun activities. Then, send home activity lists of ideas to support children's fine motor skills using typical household items. Here are some fun ideas to get you started:

- Create a simple sensory bin in a take-out container. Add dry rice, and have children scoop it with a spoon into a cup.
- Teach a teddy bear or doll how to eat with a spoon.
- Add water and food coloring to cornstarch in a container to make goopy slime.
- Squirt some shaving cream into the tub during a bath and slather it on the tile, then practice writing letters in it.
- Sort small items such as toys, cotton balls, or game pieces into a muffin tin or cups using tongs.
- Paint with water on paper using a cotton swab cut in half.
- Pour water from a medicine cup into an ice-cube tray without spilling to make ice cubes.
- Squeeze glue onto a piece of paper, and sprinkle salt on the glue. Once it dries, use paint with a brush or cotton swab to color the salt.

- Find a pinecone, interesting stone, leaf, or short stick. Dip it in paint and use it as a stamp to make impressions on paper.
- Use cookie cutters in playdough.
- Knead pizza dough before baking.
- Pick up cotton balls with tweezers and put them into a container.
- Cut paper straws with child-safe scissors.
- Push chenille stems into the holes of a kitchen strainer.
- Squeeze water from sponges into cups in the bathtub.

Host a Fine Motor Night during an Open House

Many families have anxiety and guilt about not engaging in more play with their children. Sometimes, they choose activities that their children are not developmentally ready for, or they have unrealistic expectations of what children can do. These attempts can end in meltdowns. Other parents can be overbearing and controlling, not allowing children to experience an opportunity at their own pace and level, which can be counterproductive to the child's progress.

To help families create more memories in which they interact successfully with their children, consider hosting a fine motor night. This is a fun way to model the kinds of activities that are age appropriate. Skip the boring lectures during open house night and set up centers and opportunities for families to play.

- **Self-portrait station:** Get out those markers, bingo dot markers, and broken crayons, and let children and their families showcase their skills to create pictures of themselves to take home as a keepsake.
- **Coloring station:** Invite families to color or design bookmarks or pictures to take home.
- **Handprints:** No need to make it messy. Have families use markers to trace around their hands on paper, use scissors to cut out the handprints, and turn them into monsters, bunnies, or other animals. Okay with messy stuff? Take everyone's handprints with paint and make a mural to hang in the classroom or to display on a bulletin board.

- **Sculpture station:** Invite families to use Model Magic or air-dry clay to make caterpillars, ornaments, or pretend sweet treats to take home. Leave some examples or photos around for inspiration.
- **Free-play station:** Set up a station with fun fine motor manipulative toys that families might not have at home. For example, provide Magna-Tiles, Squigz, Clixo pieces, Unifix cubes, puzzles, pop tubes, snap blocks, and gears.

This is a perfect time to showcase all the meaningful things you do in the classroom that can make a difference in a child's fine motor skills. Plus, you might inspire families to do these activities at home.

Appendix A: Toy Resources

Many different toy companies have been designing and creating educational toys that enhance fine motor skills for decades. A key advantage of these companies is their compliance with stringent safety standards in the United States. Be cautious and selective when purchasing toys and games from sites such as Amazon or Temu. Many overseas companies produce knockoff versions of popular toys. These may not match the original toys' quality and can lead to children's frustration if the toys do not work as advertised.

Toy Companies

Following is a list of excellent, trustworthy companies to consider when looking for new toys to use at home, in classrooms, and in therapy practices. Note that some of these companies might not sell their toys in local retail stores. Individual stores and websites have control over what they buy for their shelves and feature on their websites. Be sure to check out these companies online—they have a lot more items than you might expect.

Arts and Crafts		
Crayola	Crazy Aaron's	Do-a-Dot Art
Games		
Blue Orange Games	Haba	Mattel
Goliath Games	Hasbro	
Manipulatives		
Clixo	Magformers	Playmobil
Guidecraft	Magna-Tiles	Tegu (magnetic wooden blocks
Lego	MegaBloks by Mattel	
Puzzles		
Fat Brain Toys	Melissa & Doug	Ravensburger

Sensory Mediums

Crazy Aaron's (Thinking Putty)	Relevant Play (Mad Mattr)	Spin Master (Kinetic Sand)
Hasbro (Play-Doh)	WeCool Toys (Butter Cloudz compound)	
PlayVisions (Play Dirt)	Schylling (NeeDoh)	

Early Childhood Play

Constructive Playthings	Kaplan Early Learning	Moluk
Educational Insights	Lakeshore Learning	PlanToys
Fat Brain Toys	Learning Resources	PlayMonster
Goki	LeapFrog	Quercetti
Guidecraft	The Learning Journey	Ravensburger
Haba	Lovevery	ThinkFun
Hape	Melissa & Doug	VTech
Hand2Mind	MindWare	Weplay

Technology

Osmo	PlayShifu	Rolling Seeds

Toy Companies for Occupational Therapists

If you are a teacher or a therapist who is purchasing toys through a school or organization that requires purchase orders, you can also consider these companies. Parents, go ahead and check these websites out, too. Many of these organizations sell unique toys and games that cater to people with special needs. Anyone can purchase from these companies, and their websites are often easier to search because the products are also grouped by skill, such as toys for bilateral coordination or hand and finger strength.

Beyond Play https://www.beyondplay.com

Fun & Function https://www.funandfunction.com

Pocket Full of Therapy https://shoponline.pfot.com

School Specialty/Abilitations https://www.schoolspecialty.com/abilitations

Southpaw Enterprises https://www.southpaw.com

Stacy's Sensory Solutions https://stacyssensorysolutions.com

Therapy Shoppe https://therapyshoppe.com

Therapro https://www.therapro.com

Appendix B: Quick-Reference List of Toys by Skill or Concept

I've spent fifteen years playing with and learning all about the best toys in the world. Here's a quick-reference list of some of my personal favorites, organized by the type of toy or the skill it promotes. If you have some money to purchase extra resources for your classroom, you can quickly choose fun items that will add opportunities for the children in the class to have valuable learning opportunities that build strength, skill, and coordination. These toys are designed by companies committed to safety and quality; some toys are listed in multiple categories.

Rattles and Teethers

Oball Rattle by Bright Starts

Massaging Action Teether by First Years

Winkel by Manhattan Toy Company

Flip and Grip Rattle by Sassy

NogginStik Developmental Light-Up Rattle by SmartNoggin

Wrist Rattles by Infantino

Cause-and-Effect Toys

Jacque the Peacock or Mortimer the Moose Clip & Go by Lamaze

Press and Glow Spinner by Bright Starts

Pop-Up Pals by Battat

Wonder Wheel by Sassy

Water Pat Mat by Infantino

Hide and Play Hedgehog Tissue Box by Guidecraft

LeapTab Touch by LeapFrog

Fine Motor Discovery Box by Kaplan Early Learning

Activity Cubes by VTech

Tumble Ball Dome by Kaplan Early Learning

Release Patterns through Dump-and-Fill Container Play

Magical Lights Fishbowl by Fisher-Price

Discovery Stackers by Kaplan Early Learning

Little People sets by Fisher-Price

Pop-a-Balls by VTech

Peekaboo Learning Farm by Learning Resources

Toddler Circle Tower Stacker by Kaplan Early Learning

InnyBin by Fat Brain Toys

Shape Sorters

Daisy Shape Sorter by Quercetti

Bop and Drop Ball Tower by Infantino

Sort and Discover Drum by VTech

See-Inside Sorting Bucket by Lakeshore Learning

Match and Roll Shape Sorter by Melissa & Doug

Shape Factory by Fat Brain Toys

Unlock the Shape! Sorting House by Lakeshore Learning

Wonder Cube by B. Toys

Plugzy by Fat Brain Toys

Stacking Toys

SpinAgain by Fat Brain Toys

Rock-a-Stack by Fisher-Price

Rainbow Stacker by Melissa & Doug

Discovery Stackers—Rainbow Arch by Kaplan Early Learning

Toddler Circle Tower Stacker by Kaplan Early Learning

Tobbles Neo by Fat Brain Toys

Tulu (by Moluk) sets by Fat Brain Toys

Building Genius (by Moluk) by Fat Brain Toys

Puzzles

Geometric Puzzle Board by Kaplan Early Learning

Peg puzzles by Melissa & Doug

Puzzle Cards by Learning Resources

Children's puzzles by Ravensburger

Floor puzzles by Kaplan Early Learning

Wooden Latches Board by Melissa & Doug

Montessori Sort and Stack Puzzles

Blocks for Release Patterns

Rubber baby blocks by B. Toys

Soft Oversized Toddler Blocks by Kaplan Early Learning

Nesting/Stacking Blocks

Magnetic Blocks by Tegu

Mega Bloks by Mattel

Duplo Building Bricks by Lego

1-inch wooden blocks

Classic Bricks by Lego

Cork blocks by Korko

Bristle blocks

Snap blocks by Kaplan Early Learning

Wooden block sets

Stringing or Lacing Activities

On the Farm Threading Game by Haba

Lacing beads by Melissa & Doug

Lacing cards

Nest and Lace Shapes by Guidecraft

Jumbo Geo Lacing and Geo Shape Lacing by Guidecraft

Pegboards

Peg a Pattern by Fat Brain Toys

Spike the Fine Motor Hedgehog by Learning Resources

My First Peg Pictures by Lakeshore Learning

Pegboards by Skoolzy

Tall-Stackers Pegs and Pegboard Set by Lauri

Chunky Peggy by Quercetti

FantaColor Design by Quercetti

Button Art Activity Set by Alex Toys

Lite-Brite by Hasbro

Tricky Tree

Get-a-Grip Pegboard by Kinsman Enterprises

Manipulatives

Magna-Tiles

Grippies Builders by Guidecraft

K'Nex by Basic Fun

Classic Bricks by Lego

Duplo Building Bricks by Lego

Lincoln Logs

Magformers

BendiBeads by Kaplan Early Learning

Playmobil

Squigz by Fat Brain Toys

Snapo Blocks by Snapo Toys

Unifix cubes

Powerclix by Guidecraft

Unit Block Marble Run by Guidecraft

PolyForm Star Connectors by Kaplan Early Learning

Oogi (by Moluk) by Fat Brain Toys

Gross Motor Activities and Games for Strength

I Can Do That! by Wonder Forge

Roll & Play by ThinkFun

The Floor Is Lava! by Goliath Games

Cranium Hullabaloo by Funko Games

Modular play systems by Stapelstein

Bilibo (by Moluk) by Fat Brain Toys

Sensory Mediums and Activities to Build Hand Strength

Play-Doh by Hasbro

Kinetic Sand by Spin Master

Butter Cloudz Compound by WeCool Toys

Thinking Putty by Crazy Aaron's

Play Dirt by PlayVisions

Playfoam by Educational Insights

Hey Clay by Trendformer Ltd.

Fluffie Stuffiez by MGA Entertainment

TheraPutty by Fabrication Enterprises, Inc.

Preschool Games for Pincer Grasp and Hand Strength

HiHo! Cherry-O by Hasbro

Pop the Pig by Goliath Games

Jumping Jack by Goliath Games

Topple by Goliath Games

Toys That Build Hand Strength

Plui Rain Cloud (by Moluk) by Fat Brain Toys

Oogi (by Moluk) by Fat Brain Toys

Handheld exercise balls

Finger poppers

Pop tubes

Mr. Potato Head by Hasbro

Pop-Up Pirate by Tomy

Activities for Index-Finger Strength and Control for Pointing

Mindful Mazes by Hand2Mind

Sensory Pads by Hand2Mind

My First Crayola Touch Lights by Crayola

Poke-a-Dot books by Melissa & Doug

Dimpl by Fat Brain Toys

Preschool Activities and Games with Tools (Tweezers, Tongs, Spatulas, Hammers)

Create & Design Drill Kit by Learning Resources

Find the Letter Activity Center by Lakeshore Learning

Fruit and Vegetable Cut-Ups by Lakeshore Learning

Pancake Pile-Up! by Educational Insights

The Sneaky, Snacky Squirrel Game! by Educational Insights

Super Sorting Pie by Learning Resources

Mini Muffin Matchup by Learning Resources

Magnetic Wands by Lakeshore Learning

Critter Clinic by B. Toys

Don't Break the Ice by Hasbro

Noodle Knockout by Learning Resources

Fishing-Pole Games for Upper-Body and Hand Strength

Let's Go Fishin' by Goliath Games

Catch and Count Fishing Game by Melissa & Doug

Shark Bite by Goliath Games

Reel Big Catch Game by Educational Insights

Visual and Perceptual Games

Spot It! by Zygomatic

Eye Found It! by Wonder Forge

Qwirkle by MindWare

Perfection by Hasbro

Animal Train Sort & Match by Guidecraft

Koala Capers by Educational Insights

Visual Motor Games

Connect 4 by Hasbro

Perfection by Hasbro

Operation by Hasbro

KerPlunk by Hasbro

Stylus Toys to Assist with Tripod Grasp Pattern

Re-Write LCD Writing/Drawing Tablets by Boogie Board

Operation Pet Scan by Hasbro

Magnetic puzzle games by Melissa & Doug

Water Wow! products by Melissa & Doug

LeapStart 3D Learning System by LeapFrog

LeapStart Go by LeapFrog

Magnatab A to Z Uppercase and Lowercase boards by Playskool

Magnatab Free Draw by Playskool

Magna Doodle by Cra-Z-Art

Aquadoodle by Spin Master

Hot Dots by Educational Insights

Spirographs

Wooly Willy

Colorful Bead Magnetic Mosaic by Kaplan Early Learning

Operation by Hasbro

Magna Tablet by Guidecraft

Big Gem Diamond Painting kits by Creativity for Kids

Fun Toys and Activities That Require Coloring or Pens

Magic Trace by WeCool Toys

Color Wonder Mess-Free Coloring products by Crayola

Water Wow! products by Melissa & Doug

Fine Motor Gadgets for Use in Sensory Play

Twisty Droppers by Learning Resources

Handy Scoopers by Learning Resources

Tri-Grip Tongs by Learning Resources

Gator Grabber Tweezers by Learning Resources

Primary Science Jumbo Tweezers by Learning Resources

Easy-Grip Tweezers by Learning Resources

Travel Games for Pincer Grasp

Connect 4 by Hasbro

Letter Games to Assist with Letter Awareness

Zingo! by ThinkFun

Boggle Jr. by Hasbro

Frida's Fruit Fiesta Game by Educational Insights

Games and Activities That Require Two Hands to Play

Rapper Snappers (also known as Pop Tubes) by Therapro

Fruit and Vegetable Cut-Ups by Lakeshore Learning

Mobi Zippee by Mobi

Snap-Block Animals by Guidecraft

Dimpl by Fat Brain Toys

Bubble Bath Whisk by Haba

Toys with Locks and Latches

Peekaboo Lock Boxes by Guidecraft

Critter Clinic by B. Toys

Wooden Latches Board by Melissa & Doug

Montessori busy boards

Visual Motor Activities with Instructions or Picture Cards

Snap-Block Animals by Guidecraft

Classic Bricks by Lego

Interlox Squares by Kaplan Early Learning

Duplo Build Me "Emotions" by Lego

PolyForm Star Connectors by Kaplan Early Learning

Twisty Tools by Kaplan Early Learning

Fantacolor Junior Pegboard by Quercetti

BendiBeads by Kaplan Early Learning

Wooden Mosaic Set with Grid by Kaplan Early Learning

Get-a-Grip Pegboard by Kinsman Enterprises

Peg a Pattern by Fat Brain Toys

Design & Drill Activity Center by Educational Insights

Easels

Wooden Tabletop Easel by Kaplan Early Learning

Floor-Style Adjustable-Height Art Easel by Kaplan Early Learning

Magnetic & Dry-Erase Tabletop Easel by Kaplan Early Learning

Self-Care Skills

Dress-up vests with closures

Appendix C: Common Items for Simple Activities

While it can be tempting to hop online or take a trip to the store to buy new toys and games to promote fine motor skills, there are so many items you may already have that can be used for activities.

If you need some ideas of activities to do, check online. Using a search engine such as Google or generative artificial intelligence (AI), you can easily search for activities that use the specific items or ingredients you have. When searching, opt to look in the categories of images and videos if you benefit from step-by-step activities and tutorials. Here are some suggested search prompts:

- Show me fine motor activities for a four-year-old using scissors, glue, craft sticks, and googly eyes
- Crafts using paper, glue, and scissors
- How to make slime or playdough with three ingredients

The following is a list of common items you might use:

Art Supplies

Chalk
Colored pencils
Corrugated cardboard
Construction paper
Craft scissors
Craft sticks
Crayons
Fabric
Feathers
Felt
Foam shapes
Foam stickers
Gel pens
Glitter
Glue bottles
Glue dots
Glue guns
Glue sticks
Googly eyes
Highlighters
Ink pads
Markers
Paints (acrylic, washable, watercolor, fingerpaint)
Paintbrushes
Pencil sharpeners
Perler beads
Chenille stems
Pompoms
Puffy paint
Rulers
Scissors
Sharpies
Stampers
Stickers
Styrofoam
Tape (double-sided, masking, clear)
Tracing paper
Washi tape
Window markers
Yarn

Bathroom

- Cotton swabs
- Cotton balls
- Hair gel
- Saline solution
- Shaving gel

Household Items

- Baking pans or cookie sheets
- Buttons
- Cardboard boxes
- Cardboard rolls (wrapping paper, paper towel)
- Clothespins
- Duct tape
- Golf tees
- Ice-cube trays
- Medicine cups
- Muffin pans
- Paint rollers
- Paper bags
- Paper baking cups
- Paper plates
- Paper towels
- Pool noodles (foam)
- Silicone molds
- Shoelaces
- Spray bottles
- Sponges
- Straws
- Take-out containers (with disposable plastic lids)

Kitchen Drawers

- Chopsticks
- Meat-baller scoops
- Mini spatulas
- Pickle pinchers
- Salad tongs
- Scoops
- Strawberry hullers
- Tea-bag infusers
- Toaster tongs

Office

- Binders (three-ring)
- Book rings (used to hold loose-leaf papers together)
- Brass fasteners
- Card stock
- Highlighters
- Hole punches (three-hole and single-hole)
- Glue sticks
- Glue bottles
- Paper clips
- Plastic page protectors
- Pushpins
- Staplers
- Tracing paper

Pantry

- Baking soda
- Beans (dried)
- Cornstarch
- Cream of tartar
- Flour
- Food coloring
- Gelatin powder
- Instant pudding
- Oil (coconut, vegetable)
- Rice
- Salt
- Uncooked pasta
- Resealable bags

Appendix D: Glossary of Terms

Ambidextrous: having the ability to use both hands equally with the same amount of well-developed skill

Beery-Buktenica Developmental Test of Visual-Motor Integration: a standardized test often given by occupational therapists and psychologists, during which children use a pencil or marker to copy different developmental shapes. The shapes must be accurate and copied with the correct size. The test can offer an age-equivalent score and results can be used as a predictor of writing readiness. If children are able to copy the first twelve shapes of this test, they have the prewriting foundational skills needed to write letters and numbers.

Bilateral coordination: the ability to use both hands in a coordinated way at the same time. One hand might stabilize the item, while the other performs the action. Or, both hands could be performing an activity simultaneously. Examples of bilateral coordination would be tying shoelaces or holding a bead in one hand and inserting a string with the other.

Commando crawling (*also* army crawling): a means of mobility by which an infant's belly touches the ground and the arms and legs are used in an alternating fashion to move the infant forward and backward

Complex rotation: the ability to hold a small item, such as a bead or a coin, in the fingertips and rotate it in clockwise and counterclockwise directions

Container baby syndrome: when infants spend too much time in devices like infant swings, portable car seats, jumpers and floor sitters, and less time engaging in supervised tummy time or play on the floor. This lack of play experience can result in weak core and upper-body strength.

Creeping: another name for what most people understand as crawling on the hands and knees; an infant moves forward on their hands and knees using alternating arm and leg motions. Reciprocal crawling or creeping is when the right hand moves forward and the left knee also moves forward simultaneously, followed by the left hand and right knee.

Digital pronate grasp: the whole hand and all five fingers grasp a tool, such as a marker or spoon, and the forearm rotates so that the thumb is positioned down toward the paper or bowl of food

Dynamic seating systems: different types of cushions and chairs for classroom seating to improve posture. Examples include air-filled cushions, wobble stools, and therapy-ball chairs.

Dynamic or mature tripod grasp pattern: thought of as the most mature, complex, and coordinated grasp pattern. The thumb, index, and middle finger support the utensil near the tip, while the ring and pinky fingers are flexed into the palm. When writing, the fingertips move, allowing control to color and write precisely in small areas.

Fine motor skills: a general term for how people use their hands to engage in everyday activities. This encompasses the skills to pick up items and use them with coordination and to perform activities that are expected for the person's age and/or stage of development.

Fingertip grasp: all five fingers grip or support a tool or utensil. The ring and pinky fingers assist in holding the tool rather than being separated and flexed into the palm.

Handedness: when a child shows a preference for, and ultimately the consistent use of, the same hand for skilled activities such as drawing, throwing, and eating

Hand over hand: a technique in which an adult places their hand on top of or over a child's hand to guide or cue them through activities to teach new skills. This is a form of physical cueing.

Index-finger isolation: another term for pointing to something with the index finger, when the remaining fingers are flexed into the palm so only the index finger is used to point or poke

In-hand manipulation: the ability to hold small items in the hand and maneuver them for use with coordination, without fumbling or dropping them; for example, picking up three coins, one at a time, holding them in the palm of the hand, then releasing them one after another into a slotted container or machine

Intrinsic muscles: the small muscles positioned in the fat pads of the hand, which are at the base of the thumb and the pinky finger. When these muscles are strong, the hand can make refined and accurate marks to write or color with control. If these muscles are weak, children generally will not use an effective grasp pattern and will fatigue or tire quickly.

Key pinch: a grasp pattern in which an item is positioned in the hand and stabilized with the thumb against the index finger. This grasp pattern is often used when strength is needed, such as inserting a key into a lock and turning it to the left or right.

Lateral grasp: holding a small piece of food, a toy, or a writing utensil, with the thumb placed on the side of the index finger. Generally, the web space, the C-shaped area between the thumb and the index finger, is closed and the whole hand works as one unit.

Lateral quadripod grasp: holding a writing tool with four fingers: the thumb, index, middle, and ring fingers. The thumb is positioned against the side of the index finger. While this is not the most mature grasp, it is considered to be a functional grasp pattern for most people.

Midline: a name for an imaginary vertical line in the center of the body. Bringing both hands to midline, such as in clapping or holding a bottle with both hands to drink, is an important developmental skill

Multifinger grasp: any combination of fingers holds a utensil. Sometimes, this can be an awkward grasp pattern, such as when the index finger is not positioned at the tip of a pencil but the finger is extended and supports the pencil near the middle or upper part of the shaft.

Palmar grasp: a primitive, early grasp pattern in which a toy is held in the hand, but the item is supported in the palm of the hand and not held with the fingertips. A palmar grasp will develop before a tripod grasp pattern.

Palmar grasp reflex: seen in infants, an automatic response from the neurological system, in which the fingers will close, or squeeze, when pressure is a applied to the palm. This reflex will lessen overtime as grasp and release patterns develop to allow for more refined fine motor control.

Physical cueing: also known as tactile cueing, this might include demonstrating what to do, gesturing, or actually maneuvering a child's hand through an activity to complete the skill

Pincer grasp: a precision grasp pattern in which the thumb and the tip of the index finger pick up small items to be used accurately. The middle, ring, and pinky fingers of the hand are flexed into the palm.

Power grip: the whole hand, or all five fingers, are needed to pick up a large item such as a large cup, the handle of a gallon jug, or a quart-size container full of liquid

Precision grip: encompasses different types of grasp patterns, including the pincer grasp or tripod grasp pattern, which are needed for accuracy and control. A precision grip uses only the fingertips of the thumb, index, and middle finger to complete activities with small items.

Pronated grasp: similar to a digital pronate grasp pattern, but instead of the fingers supporting the tool, the item is held tightly in the palm of the hand while the thumb is rotated down toward the paper. This is an early grasp pattern that toddlers often use, which will generally develop into a quadripod-style and ultimately a tripod-style grasp pattern over time.

Radial digital grasp: smaller items like toys, blocks, beads, or food are held in the fingertips, generally with the thumb, index, and middle finger. These three fingers are on the radial side of the hand—the side that the thumb is on—and are innervated by the radial nerve.

Raking grasp: an immature grasp pattern that babies often use first, around eight months of age, when they try to pick up small food items to feed themselves. The pinky side of the hand is positioned on the surface, and the fingers attempt to pick up the food with a sweeping, uncoordinated action.

Reflex: an involuntary movement or response that comes from the brain and the neurological system to make the body move automatically. Reflexes will *integrate*, or disappear, over time, but are initially present for survival. For example, the rooting reflex is when a person strokes the side of an infant's mouth, and the infant turns their head to that side and opens their mouth to accept a nipple to eat (bottle or breast).

Release patterns: the skill of letting go of items with control, to place items into a container or on a surface. This skill is needed to position puzzles into a form board or shapes into a shape sorter, to stack blocks, or to place a small item into a twist-off container.

Separation of the hand: the fine motor development of the hand to use a power grip with all five fingers, then transition this grasp into a precision grip in which the thumb, index, and middle fingers are used while the ring and pinky fingers are flexed into the palm. Grasp patterns that include separation of the hand are needed for strength and coordination.

Shift: the ability to hold the end of an item and to use the fingertips to move the item forward and back, to adjust it into a different position. This skill includes holding a pencil in the middle of the shaft and moving the fingers to transition the fingers down near the tip, or using the fingertips to turn the pages of a book.

Simple rotation: ability to hold small items and twist them. This is the skill needed to twist off the cap of a container or to turn the knob of a wind-up toy.

Stabilizing hand: another name for the nondominant hand when it's used to hold an item securely while the dominant hand performs an action; also known as the "helper hand"

Static tripod grasp: using a hand to hold a tool with the thumb, index, and middle fingers, but the fingers are not dynamic, which means they do not move when writing or coloring; the movement and control is often initiated from the wrist and the hand moves as a unit

Three-jaw chuck grasp: a grasp pattern often needed for strength, in which the index and middle fingers are placed on the top of an item and the thumb is placed underneath. This grasp pattern is often used to squeeze a clothespin or to seal a plastic storage bag.

Translation: an in-hand manipulation skill, in which items like food, beads, or coins are stored in the palm of the hand, then the thumb slides across the remaining fingers to move the item from the palm into the fingertips; also known as palm-to-finger translation. Finger-to-palm translation is when an item in the fingertips is moved back into the palm.

Tripod-style grasp: a general name for either a dynamic or static tripod grasp, which uses the thumb, index, and middle fingers to support the tool or utensil

Verbal cueing: using words to offer encouragement, speak directions, use short phrases, or sing songs to help guide a child to a better performance and to learn new skills. Cueing is best with clear and concise directions. An example would be saying, "Do this," or singing, "Open, shut them; open, shut them," to help a child learn to open and close their scissors.

Visual-motor skills: relates to the activities completed with skill and coordination after an item is grasped and picked up for use; for example, picking up a pencil and writing a name, placing a pair of scissors on the hands to cut out a circle, or manipulating the buttons on a shirt to get dressed

Web space: the C-shaped space in the hand where a pencil rests when using a tripod-style grasp with the fingertips

References and Recommended Reading

Almasri, Nihad A., Mihee An, and Robert J. Palisano. 2018. "Parents' Perception of Receiving Family-Centered Care for their Children with Physical Disabilities: A Meta-Analysis." *Physical and Occupational Therapy in Pediatrics* 38(4): 427–443.

Alotaibi, Thekra, et al. 2020. "The Relationship between Technology Use and Physical Activity among Typically Developing Children." *Healthcare* 8(4): 488.

Avruskin, Andrea. 2018. "Physical-Therapy Guide to Container Baby Syndrome." ChoosePT. https://www.choosept.com/guide/physical-therapy-guide-container-baby-syndrome

Bassok, Daphna, Scott Latham, and Anna Rorem. 2016. "Is Kindergarten the New First Grade?" *AERA Open* 1(4): 1–33. https://files.eric.ed.gov/fulltext/EJ1194581.pdf

Beery, Keith E., Norman A. Buktenica, and Natasha A. Beery. 2010. *Beery-Buktenica Developmental Test of Visual-Motor Integration.* 6th ed. Minneapolis, MN: Pearson.

Bos, Arend, F., et al. 2013. "Development of Fine Motor Skills in Preterm Infants." *Developmental Medicine and Child Neurology* 55(Supp. 4): 1–4.

Case-Smith, Jane. 1995. "The Relationships among Sensorimotor Components, Fine Motor Skill, and Functional Performance in Preschool Children." *American Journal of Occupational Therapy* 49(7): 645–652.

Case-Smith, Jane, and Jane C. O'Brien. 2015. *Occupational Therapy for Children and Adolescents.* 7th ed. St. Louis, MO: Elsevier Mosby.

Centers for Disease Control and Prevention. 2023a. CDC's Developmental Milestones. CDC.gov. https://www.cdc.gov/ncbddd/actearly/milestones/index.html

Centers for Disease Control and Prevention. 2023b. "Data and Statistics About ADHD." Attention-Deficit/Hyperactivity Disorder (ADHD). https://www.cdc.gov/ncbddd/adhd/data.html

Common Sense Media. 2013. *Zero to Eight: Children's Media Use in America 2013*. https://www.commonsensemedia.org/sites/default/files/research/report/zero-to-eight-2013.pdf

Corey, David M., Megan M. Hurley, and Anne L. Foundas. 2001. "Right- and Left-Handedness Defined: A Multivariate Approach Using Hand Preference and Hand Performance Measures." *Neuropsychiatry, Neuropsychology, and Behavioral Neurology* 14(3): 144–152.

Đurišić, Maša, and Mila Bunijevac. 2017. "Parent Involvement as an Important Factor for Successful Education." *Center for Educational Policy Studies Journal* 7(3): 137–153.

Engel, Courtney, Kristin Lillie, Sarah Zurawski, and Brittany G. Travers. 2018. "Curriculum-Based Handwriting Programs: A Systematic Review with Effect Sizes." *American Journal of Occupational Therapy* 72(3): 7203205010p1–7203205010p8.

Engelen, Lina, et al. 2013. "Increasing Physical Activity in Young Primary Schoolchildren—It's Child's Play: A Cluster Randomised Controlled Trial." *Preventive Medicine* 56(5): 319–325.

Harmon, Flora, and Radhika Viruru. 2018. "Debunking the Myth of the Efficacy of 'Push-Down Academics': How Rigid, Teacher-Centered, Academic Early Learning Environments Disempower Young Children." *Journal of Family Strengths* 18(1). https://digitalcommons.library.tmc.edu/jfs/vol18/iss1/11

Hee Chung, Estefani, Jesse Chou, and Kelly A. Brown. 2020. "Neurodevelopmental Outcomes of Preterm Infants: A Recent Literature Review." *Translational Pediatrics* 9(Supp. 1): S3–S8.

Henderson, Anne, and Charlane Pehoski, eds. 2006. *Hand Function in the Child: Foundations for Remediation*. 2nd ed. St. Louis, MO: Mosby.

Huffman, J. Michelle, and Callie Fortenberry. 2011. "Helping Preschoolers Prepare for Writing: Developing Fine Motor Skills." *Young Children* 66(5): 100, 102–103.

Kılıç, Mahmut, and Şeyda Koçak. 2023. "Examination of Psycho-Motor Development of Children Who Were 6–36 Months in the COVID-19 Stay-at-Home Period." *Scientific Reports* 13(1): 20801.

Kretch, Kari S., et al. 2022. "'Learn the Signs. Act Early': Updates and Implications for Physical Therapists." *Pediatric Physical Therapy* 34(4): 440–448.

Longhine, Laura. 2022. "Play-Based Learning vs. Academics in Preschool." *US News and World Report*, June 17. https://www.usnews.com/education/k12/articles/play-based-learning-vs-academics-in-preschool

McCleskey, Jan. 2019. *Development of a Fine Motor Program for Classrooms and Occupational Therapy*. Richardson, TX: The Handwriting Clinic. https://www.thehandwritingclinic.com/CM/Brochures/Files/2019%20%20Developing%20a%20Fine%20Motor%20Program%20for%20Children.pdf

Martinez, LaQuita, David C. Dugdale, and Brenda Conaway. 2023. "Fetal Development." *MedlinePlus Medical Encyclopedia*. https://medlineplus.gov/ency/article/002398.htm

Michael Cohen Group. 2014. *Toys, Learning, and Play Summit: Touch Screens*. https://www.mcgrc.com/wp-content/uploads/2015/03/MCGRC_Digital-Kids-Presentation_022014.pdf

Moyer, Melinda W. 2020. "Early Education Is More Demanding Than Ever, and Experts Have Concerns." *The New York Times*, April 17. https://www.nytimes.com/2020/04/17/parenting/early-childhood-education-demands.html

Obradović, Jelena, Michael J. Sulik, and Anne Shafer. 2021. "Learning to Let Go: Parental Over-Engagement Predicts Poorer Self-Regulation in Kindergartners." *Journal of Family Psychology* 35(8): 1160–1170.

Olsen, Jan, and Emily Knapton. 2008. *Handwriting Without Tears Pre-K Teachers Guide*. 4th ed. Cabin John, MD: Handwriting Without Tears.

Park, Jung Ha, et al. 2020. "Sedentary Lifestyle: Overview of Updated Evidence of Potential Health Risks." *Korean Journal of Family Medicine* 41(6): 365–373.

Posar, Annio, and Paola Visconti. 2022. "Early Motor Signs in Autism Spectrum Disorder." *Children-Basel* 9(2): 294.

Rideout, Victoria, and Michael B. Robb. 2020. *The Common Sense Census: Media Use by Kids Age Zero to Eight*. San Francisco, CA: Common Sense Media. https://www.commonsensemedia.org/sites/default/files/research/report/2020_zero_to_eight_census_final_web.pdf

Ross, Elizabeth M. 2023. "Embracing Artificial Intelligence in the Classroom." Harvard Graduate School of Education. Last updated July 20, 2023. https://www.gse.harvard.edu/ideas/usable-knowledge/23/07/embracing-artificial-intelligence-classroom

Saint-Maurice, Pedro F., et al. 2017. "Impact of NFL PLAY 60 Programming on Elementary School Children's Body Mass Index and Aerobic Capacity: The NFL PLAY 60 FitnessGram Partnership Project." *Journal of School Health* 87(11): 873–881.

Schwellnus, Heidi, et al. 2012. "Effect of Pencil Grasp on the Speed and Legibility of Handwriting in Children." *American Journal of Occupational Therapy* 66(6): 718–726.

Sha, Zhiquiang, et al. 2021. "Handedness and Its Genetic Influences Are Associated with Structural Asymmetries of the Cerebral Cortex in 31,864 Individuals." *Proceedings of the National Academy of Sciences of the United States of America* 118(47): e2113095118. doi: 10.1073/pnas.2113095118

Skene, Kayleigh, et al. 2022. "Can Guidance during Play Enhance Children's Learning and Development in Educational Contexts? A Systematic Review and Meta-Analysis." *Child Development* 93(4): 1162–1180.

Takahashi, Ippei, et al. 2023. "Screen Time at Age 1 Year and Communication and Problem-Solving Developmental Delay at 2 and 4 Years." *JAMA Pediatrics* 177(10): 1039–1046.

Taylor, Meaghan E., and Wanda Boyer. 2020. "Play-Based Learning: Evidence-Based Research to Improve Children's Learning Experiences in the Kindergarten Classroom." *Early Childhood Education Journal* 48(10): 127–133.

Tsimis, Michael E., Nebras Abu Al-Hamayel, H. Germaine, and Irina Burd. 2015. "Prematurity: Present and Future." *Minerva Ginecologica* 67(1): 35–46.

Watts, Rachel, and Jyotsna Pattnaik. 2022. "Perspectives of Parents and Teachers on the Impact of the COVID-19 Pandemic on Children's Socio-Emotional Well-Being." *Early Childhood Education Journal* 51(8): 1–12.

Wolraich, Mark L., et al. 2019. "Clinical Practice Guideline for the Diagnosis, Evaluation, and Treatment of Attention-Deficit/Hyperactivity Disorder in Children and Adolescents." *Pediatrics* 144(4): e20192528.

Zubler, Jennifer M., et al. 2022. "Evidence-Informed Milestones for Developmental Surveillance Tools." *Pediatrics* 149(3): e2021052138.

Index

I

J

K

L

M

N

O

U

V

W

Y

Z